Catopedia

🐾 A FASCINATING COLLECTION OF 🐾

FELINE CURIOSITIES

— FROM —

BATTERSEA
DOGS & CATS HOME

(WITH) JUSTINE HANKINS

headline

First published in 2016
by HEADLINE PUBLISHING GROUP

1

Cataloguing in Publication Data is available from the British Library

Hardback ISBN 978 1 4722 2478 1

Designed by Laura Hall

Printed and bound in Great Britain by
Clays Ltd, St Ives plc

Produced under licence from Battersea Dogs Home Ltd. R Battersea Dogs & Cats Home.

Royalties from the sale of this book go towards supporting the work of Battersea Dogs & Cats
Home. Reg charity no: 206394

Battersea Dogs & Cats Home has been caring for and rehoming abandoned, stray and neglected
animals since 1860. We have looked after 3 million dogs and cats since then and we aim never to
turn away an animal in need of our help. To find out more about the charity visit
battersea.org.uk

Headline's policy is to use papers that are natural, renewable and recyclable products and made
from wood grown in sustainable forests. The logging and manufacturing processes are expected to
conform to the environmental regulations of the country of origin.

HEADLINE PUBLISHING GROUP
An Hachette UK Company
Carmelite House
50 Victoria Embankment
London EC4Y 0DZ

www.headline.co.uk
www.hachette.co.uk

Acknowledgements

Many thanks to Conor Goold,
whose expertise and enthusiasm for
both science and companion animals
have been invaluable, and to the staff at
Battersea Dogs & Cats Home for their
help in compiling this book.

Justine Hankins, July 2016

CONTENTS

INTRODUCTION

In 1860, when she rented a disused stableyard to open what would one day become the world-famous Battersea Dogs & Cats Home, Mrs Mary Tealby made a solemn promise: she would never turn away an animal in need. That's a promise the Home still aims to keep today, over 3.1million cats and dogs later.

Battersea has three rehoming centres – in south London, at Brands Hatch in Kent, and at Old Windsor in Berkshire. The Home's vision is a world where every cat and dog has a safe and loving home. Battersea rescues, reunites and rehomes – and also works hard to educate the public about responsible pet ownership, including microchipping, neutering and welfare.

Battersea has been looking after cats since 1883 and more cats than dogs were rehomed for the second time in 2015. That year, Battersea looked after more than 8,000 lost, unwanted and abandoned animals, giving them a place of safety and the highest standards of care and welfare until a loving new home could be found.

Battersea's history

1860 – The Temporary Home for Lost & Starving Dogs is set up by Mrs Mary Tealby in a disused stableyard in Holloway, North London

1871 – The Temporary Home moves to a new site in Battersea, where it has remained ever since

1883 – Battersea starts taking in cats

1885 – Queen Victoria becomes the Home's first Royal Patron

1898 – Due to a rabies epidemic in London the Duke and Duchess of Portland open the Home's first country site in Hackbridge, Surrey (now closed)

1956 – Queen Elizabeth II becomes the Home's patron

1960 – Battersea celebrates its centenary

1979 – Battersea acquires Bell Mead Kennels on the edge of Old Windsor

1998 – The BBC films the first of four documentary series on the Home

2000 – Battersea's third centre, at Brands Hatch in Kent, is opened

2002 – The name changes to Battersea Dogs & Cats Home

2010 – Battersea opens state-of-the-art cattery at London centre

2015 – Her Majesty The Queen officially opens Battersea's Mary Tealby kennels

COMING HOME
How the cat was tamed

Cats have lived alongside us for perhaps as long as 9000 years. The elusive and solitary wildcat, *Felis sylvestris*, gradually morphed into our familiar friend, *Felis catus*, with very little human intervention. Other domestic animals have to be selectively bred or carefully trained before they become useful to humans (horses need to be broken in, cows are selected for milk yields and dogs are trained to fetch dead ducks). Cats, however, will hunt rodents whether we want them to or not and they don't need any lessons from us. These exceptional natural abilities explain why we haven't bothered much with trying to breed cats into different shapes and sizes or trained them to do various tasks. Because of this, cats have changed just enough to settle down happily in our company while retaining many characteristics of their wild ancestors.

Meet the ancestors

All species of wildcat are so closely related to domestic cats that they can interbreed, but it is *Felis sylvestris lybica*, the African wildcat (or a variety of it, sometimes called the Near Eastern wildcat), which we have to thank for our feline friends. This wildcat sub-species is believed to be the direct ancestor of all the domestic cats which live with us today. Lighter and slighter than their thick-furred European counterparts, African wildcats look a lot like our cats. They are roughly the same size and they are often tabby, although they tend to have longer legs than domestic cats.

These cats have an extensive range which takes in much of North Africa as well as the fringes of the Arabian Peninsula and the region known as the Fertile Crescent. This last detail is significant because the Fertile Crescent  (which covers much of what we know as the Middle East today) is where agriculture began. With agriculture came human settlements and then the domestication of a number of species, including sheep, goats and, perhaps more surprisingly, cats.

These early farming communities had rubbish heaps and grain stores (which attracted rodents), which clearly appealed to cats. Some wildcats seem to have managed to overcome their natural wariness towards humans and approached these settlements looking for food. Cats with a reduced fear towards humans would have been more successful at helping themselves to this plentiful food supply, and would have gone on to reproduce more successfully than timid cats. Eventually, a new type of cat emerged. Still more or less the same physically but different in one crucial respect – these new, less fearful cats had come to terms (possibly even terms of affection) with people.

A cat by any other name

Cat classification (or taxonomy) has been subject to much change and dispute, partly because wildcats are so similar, making it hard to know where to draw the lines. The number of recognised sub-species of the wildcat family has varied between five and twenty-four, depending on who was counting. African wildcat (*Felis sylvestris lybica*) has long been the name given to the sub-species which is believed to be the direct ancestor of the domestic cat, but more recently the term Near Eastern wildcat has also been used (although, whatever their English name, they are still *Felis sylvestris lybica*).

There's confusion, too, about what to call pet cats. *Felis Catus* and *Felis silvestris catus* are both used, and they have also been called Felis domesticus by those who saw domestication as a key characteristic. Whatever you call them and however you choose to separate them, all wildcats (and, indeed, their domestic relatives) are essentially the same. They can interbreed and their physiology and biology differs only in superficial aspects.

KITIONARY CORNER

Kitten, n. /ˈkɪtən/
This word has been used to describe a juvenile cat since the fourteenth century and probably came into Middle English from the Old French word *chitoun* or *cheton*, meaning a small cat.

The odd couple

You don't expect a mouse to do a cat a favour, but the house cat may never have come about if it hadn't been for the house mouse. Settled farming meant that people could produce a surplus of food so they'd have something stored away for later. This led to grain stores which, in turn, led to infestations of mice. Much like cats, these tiny rodents had previously kept well away from humans, but large quantities of unguarded grain coupled with warm, dry places to build nests tempted them into a change of lifestyle. Following hot on their little heels came cats who, in spite of their natural aversion to company, were enticed into closer contact with humans by the promise of an easy meal.

The rise of the house mouse coincides with the earliest evidence of cat domestication and it has been suggested that this change in mouse behaviour was the single most significant factor in turning the wildcat into the pet cat. It's not too far-fetched to say that mice, rather than humans, are responsible for domesticating the cat. The cat's keen work around the granary also explains why humans tolerated, even encouraged, the presence of these animals near their homes. These days, the house mouse, much like cats (whether pet or feral), almost always lives around people and both species have carved out a niche for themselves where they are at once dependent on people but also retain a degree of independence.

Island hopping

The ancient Egyptians often get the credit for domesticating the cat and they were, indeed, massive fans of all things feline. Members of this extraordinary civilization did the modern historian a huge favour by leaving such an extensive range of artefacts. When it comes to cats, we have statues, wall paintings, descriptions written in hieroglyphics and even thousands upon thousands of mummified bodies. The beginning of ancient Egypt takes us back to 3100 BC but there is evidence that the cat became domesticated even before the first Pharaoh took a stroll along the Nile.

It's no simple thing to pinpoint exactly when domestication occurred because wildcats and pet cats are so similar. Should an archaeologist unearth the remains of a long-dead cat, there's nothing about the skeleton itself which tells us definitively whether the animal was wild or tame. Unless, that is, the skeleton is found on an island which has never had a wildcat population. That's why the discovery of cat remains on the island of Cyprus (which has no indigenous wildcats) was so significant. Cats must have arrived on the island by boat so the find suggests a connection between cats and people which is much older than previously thought. These seafaring cats could, of course, have been wild animals, but wild cats would not have made for easy cabin companions so it seems much more probable that they were already domesticated.

One Cypriot cat skeleton in particular, discovered in 2004, is particularly intriguing. Believed to be about 9500 years old, the remains were found next to the grave of a human. The cat appears to have been carefully placed in the same position as the person and was found in the same state of preservation, suggesting a prompt and deliberate burial. We don't know why the pair were buried so close together (the cat could have been a companion to the afterlife or an offering to the gods) but the graves offer a tantalising glimpse of the very early days of an enduring relationship.

The cat's mother

Recent research on feline DNA suggests that all our pet cats may be descended from a few families of wildcats that live near the Tigris and Euphrates rivers in what is now Iraq and was once known as Mesopotamia (an ancient civilization right at the heart of the Fertile Crescent). DNA samples taken from wildcats in the region were compared with samples from domestic cats in order to build a feline family tree. This is achieved by comparing the cats' mitochondrial DNA (passed on through the maternal line), which provides information about the evolutionary relationships between different species. Researchers working on the project believe it's possible that the lineage leading to today's cats may have started in the wildcat population somewhere between 70,000 and 100,000 years ago. Humans began settling in the area around 10,000 years ago - which is possibly when this line of cats made their first steps towards sharing a home with us.

Chinese puzzle

The riddle of exactly where and when the cat was first domesticated may never be solved and in some ways the more we learn, the more questions we unearth. Recent excavations in China have brought to light some very old cat remains, which brings into question some long-held suppositions about the origins of the cat. It's widely accepted that cat domestication first took place in the Middle East or North Africa, which is a very long way from China. Yet feline bones, believed to be around 5300 years old, were recently found at the site of an ancient village in the Chinese province of Shaanxi.

It's impossible to say whether these cats were wild or domestic, but specialist analysis of the bone material suggests the cats feasted on mice that had eaten farmed millet. In other words, these cats must have lived in close proximity to humans. At least one of the cats appears to have been quite old, suggesting life in the village wasn't too bad. Archaeologists also found evidence of significant rodent damage to storage areas, so the cats may well have been very welcome.

Unfortunately, researchers were not able to find enough DNA in the bone fragments to identify which species the cats belonged to, so it's not yet known if these cats were introduced from elsewhere or if they represent an additional and unrelated occurrence of domestication.

Cross-Channel cats

The Romans certainly made their mark on the world. In the wake of their frequent invading and colonising they left behind some very useful stuff. Straight roads, for a start, and paved streets and aqueducts. They also had a hand in spreading the domestic cat across much of western Europe, including Britain. When the Romans invaded Britain in 55, 54 and then again in 43 BC, they brought cats with them. Cat remains have been found at Roman sites in Essex and Kent and cat paw prints have been discovered on Roman tiles in Gloucester and Shropshire.

But were Roman cats really the first domestic felines to arrive on these shores? Given that no cat is ever going to swim across the Channel, someone must have brought them here (our own indigenous wildcats are far too wild to be tamed). But lots of invaders and traders had already crossed the sea by the time the Romans got here. One intriguing find in the Dorset village of Gussage All Saints points to the possibility that the cat arrived in Britain even before the Romans. The bones of seven cats (five of them kittens), dating from around 250 BC, were found at an Iron Age fort. The fact that the cats were obviously breeding so near to human dwellings suggests they were not wild. Tellingly, some of the earliest evidence of house mice in Britain was also found at the site. Bones will keep their secrets and we may never get to the bottom of exactly when domestic cats first arrived in Britain but these skeletal remains appear to underline an ancient truth – cats and humans are drawn to each other because people hate mice and cats love them – for dinner, that is.

Taming your little tiger

Domestication has only touched the surface of the cat – at heart they remain fundamentally the same as their wild ancestors. This wild streak is undoubtedly part of their charm. Cats are regarded as free-spirited creatures and admired for their apparent independence. But nobody wants a cat that really behaves like a tiger in the house, which might be exactly what you'll get without some timely and kindly interaction with kittens. The fact is that, even after many centuries of living alongside humans, cats are not natural-born, docile, domestic pets. They do, however, differ from their wild cousins in one crucial respect – they have an inborn capacity to learn how to be amenable companions.

In order for this to happen, though, they need a sound upbringing. Between two and seven weeks of age, kittens experience a 'socialisation period'. This is when they are curious about the world around them, open to new experiences and are unafraid of the unfamiliar. It's vital that kittens at this stage of life have plenty of positive experiences of being near people. Kittens who are not frequently handled during this phase may develop an exaggerated fear response which is likely to stay with them throughout adulthood. While cats will always be partly wild at heart, they do need a little help to become tame enough to be content in our company.

WILDCATS TODAY

Meet the relatives

Cats are members of the *felidae* family, which includes the big cats as well as a number of much smaller species. In fact, the majority of wild cats are much closer in size to our own domestic pets than they are to lions and tigers. All wild cats are carnivorous hunters and most are solitary, elusive creatures, making them difficult to study. Most cat species, including the domestic cat's nearest relative, the African wildcat, are under threat from habitat loss and their numbers are in decline. Many millions of domestic cats, on the other hand, have returned to a semi-wild state and there are colonies of feral cats all over the world.

What is a wildcat?

There are wild cats and wildcats – which is a little confusing. A wild cat is just a cat that is wild. So that's a cheetah or a leopard or an ocelot, say. Whereas a wildcat is *Felis silvestris*, the species most closely related to domestic cats (*Felis catus*). There are African, Asiatic and European wildcats (of which the Scottish wildcat is a sub-species) and they live in a wide variety of habitats, from the forests of Europe to the savannahs of Africa.

Last fling for the Highland tiger?

At first glance, a Scottish wildcat looks quite a lot like a large and not especially friendly tabby. They are, in fact, hardy predators and ill-suited to a life curled up in front of the fire. In fact, it's not possible to tame them at all, despite their extremely close resemblance to their domestic cousins. Catching a glimpse of one of these elusive creatures is no easy task, as they live in remote areas and tend to keep well away from humans. Counting them is further complicated by the fact that it takes an experienced eye to tell a true wildcat apart from a domestic tabby.

Wildcats were living in the British Isles long before the arrival of the domestic cat, but their forest habitat dramatically decreased over the centuries, as wild spaces were turned into agricultural land. Hunted for their fur during the Middle Ages and well into the 18th century, the persecution of wildcats reached a peak during the Victorian age, when shooting became a popular pastime for well-to-do gentlemen. Wildcats were considered a threat to game birds, so gamekeepers were paid a bounty for every cat killed and their bodies were hung up on public display as evidence of the gamekeeper's diligence. The species is now on the brink of extinction and there may be fewer than 100 true Scottish wildcats living in the wild. Now a protected species, they are still at considerable risk from hybridisation (by interbreeding with domestic or feral cats), disease (particularly parasites and infections spread by feral cats) and road traffic. Conservation plans are in place to protect the surviving population, but it remains to be seen whether it's too late to save Britain's last surviving wildcats.

KITIONARY CORNER

Tom, n. /tɒm/

Tom or tomcat was first recorded as the name for a male cat in 1809 and was possibly influenced by a children's book called *The Life and Adventures of a Cat*, published in 1760, which was about a cat called Tom. Previously, male cats had been known as gib-cats (since 1400) as well as boar-cats and ram-cats.

TEN LITTLE CAT SPECIES

Big cats tend to steal the show when it comes to wildlife documentaries, but little cats are just as fascinating as lions or tigers. They often live in remote areas and can be very hard to spot – which is why they remain something of a mystery, even to dedicated naturalists. Here are ten small cat species that you rarely hear about.

Rusty-spotted cat (*Prionailurus rubiginosus*): This tiny feline lives in India and Sri Lanka and is one of the smallest cats in the world, weighing around 1.5 kilograms and standing at 30cm (12in). It's been reported that some of these cats have made a home for themselves in derelict buildings near urban areas.

Pallas's cat (*Otocolobus manul*): These stocky, long-coated, flat-faced cats live mainly in inaccessible regions of Central Asia and they stalk their prey around rock crevices and burrows. They are named after the German naturalist Peter Simon Pallas, who first identified the species in 1776.

Sand cat (*Felis margarita*): This cat survives in the arid terrain of the Sahara as well as desert regions in Asia. They get most of their fluids from food (mainly gerbils) and have specially adapted feet which barely leave a footprint in the sand.

Black-footed cat (*Felis nigripes*): No bigger than your average pet cat, this is the smallest cat in Africa. Their coats are a bold, spotted pattern and the soles of their feet are black, which protects them from the heat of the hot sand.

Flat-headed cat (*Prionailurus planiceps*): As its name suggests, this rare wild cat has an unusually shaped, flattened forehead. They live in wetlands in Borneo, Sumatra and Malaysia and have partially webbed toes, which are a great help when hunting fish.

Marbled cat (*Pardofelis marmorata*): This beautifully patterned cat looks like a miniature clouded leopard, with all its swirls, spots and stripes. They live in tropical forests in Southeast Asia and feed on tree-dwelling mammals. They are very elusive and have rarely been studied in the wild.

Andean cat (*Leopardus jacobita*): These thick-coated cats live in the high terrain of the Andes Mountains. Mass over-hunting of chinchillas for their fur has deprived the Andean cat of a significant food source and has made it the most threatened cat species in the Americas.

Jaguarundi (*Puma yagouaroundi*): This unusual-looking cat has short ears, a flattened head and a tail like an otter's. They are often active during daylight hours and their range extends across Central and South America, from Mexico to Uruguay. Unlike many cats, they are frequently observed travelling in pairs.

Pampas cat (*Leopardus pajeros*): These wild cats are easily mistaken for domestic cats and live in a greater range of habitats than any other feline in Latin America. They can survive in grassland, woodland, swamps and forests. They have not been extensively studied in the wild so not a great deal is known about their hunting habits.

African golden cat (*Caracal aurata*): About twice the size of a domestic cat, this elusive, solitary feline lives in the forests of Equatorial Africa. They share much of the same range as leopards, but very little is known about them. No one had even managed to photograph one of these secretive felines in the wild until 2002.

And one case of mistaken identity

Civets and their relatives are sometimes called civet cats. They do, after all, look a bit like cats and have spotty, tabby coats. They are actually more closely related to meerkats and mongooses and are not part of the feline family.

Back to nature

While many species of wild cats, both big and small, are struggling to survive, one group of felines can multiply like nobody's business if left to their own devices. Feral cats are domesticated cats that can get by without human help and have to live on their wits. They survive largely by scavenging around humans (although they generally like to keep their distance), with a bit of hunting thrown in.

What's remarkable about feral cats is that these naturally solitary animals often co-exist in large groups – although, inevitably, catfights and squabbles do break out from time to time. Most feral colonies are centred around groups of related females and their kittens. The size of the colony seems largely determined but the amount of food available. Where food is limited, some families will be forced out, but where food is in plentiful supply, many hundreds of cats may be able to live together more or less peacefully.

Domestic cats breed far more often than wild cats, so feral colonies can quickly become over-populated. It's impossible to say exactly how many feral cats there are in the world, but it's thought to be in the tens of millions. There are feral cat populations in both urban and rural areas, in rich countries and poor ones, and in all sorts of different environments. Controlling feral cat populations is no easy feat either. Where cats are removed, they are usually quickly replaced by more.

Life in a feral cat colony holds some fascination for those studying feline behaviour. The group dynamics reveal an adaptability in the domestic cat which is rarely observed in their wild cousins, who are generally much more set in their ways. From an animal welfare perspective, however, feral cats are a cause for concern. Given the intense competition for food, coupled with the prevalence of parasites and disease, life for a feral cat can be harsh and short. In order to deal with the problem, many welfare organisations run trap, neuter, return (TNR) programmes, a humane and effective way to control feral populations. Once neutered, the feral cat (distinguished by having its left ear tipped) is returned back to its colony or territory.

THE CAT'S BODY

The remarkable physiology of the domestic cat

Cats are amazing creatures with athletic abilities far beyond anything a human could manage, as anyone who's ever tried to catch a mouse can appreciate. Cats can jump and climb and squeeze through tiny spaces, and generally navigate their way around a three-dimensional world with much greater ease and dexterity than humans and many other mammals. In order to do this, they have some very special physical features which make them supremely well-adapted to early-morning escapades and late-evening prowling.

Seeing things

The eyes of a cat are relatively large compared to those of other mammals. With their dilating irises, which appear to wax and wane like the moon, and their reflective 'glow in the dark' properties, they have a magical aspect which has fascinated humans for centuries. Even when we're armed with the science explaining exactly how the feline eye operates, it is difficult to imagine quite how cats experience their visual world because it differs in some crucial ways to our own.

Cats have a wider field of vision than humans – call it a widescreen effect – which gives them more peripheral vision than us, so they can get a proper look at something that we might just glimpse out of the corner of our eye, if we're lucky. The cat's eye also makes the most of every scrap of light, so their night vision is much better than ours. But there is a trade-off. Cats are not as good as us at focusing on close objects – so if it's right under their nose, it's just a blur.

Nor do cats have much time for colour. They don't actually see in black and white, but they only have two types of cones (cells in the retina which are sensitive to colour), one green-sensitive and one blue-sensitive. Humans have three types of cones, so we can distinguish a greater range of colours. In any case, cats are not wired to give much importance to colour, so everything else about an object – its size, shape, movement and the amount of light it gives off – gets much more attention from the feline brain.

One feature the cat has that we manage without is something called the nictitating membrane, which is a kind of third, semi-transparent eyelid. Common in birds and reptiles, this extra feature gives the cat added protection and keeps the eye moist, so they don't need to blink as much as we do.

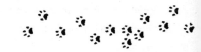

Kept in the dark

Contrary to popular belief, cats can't actually see in the dark. That's to say, if it's absolutely pitch black, a cat is just as likely to stumble over a discarded cat toy as we are. But their vision in dim light is many times better than ours – ideal for a spot of hunting at dusk. Their large, elliptical pupils can open very wide to allow in as much light as possible. Cats also have a reflective layer of cells behind the retina, called the *tapetum lucidum*, which acts as a mirror and reflects light onto the retina, boosting night vision and creating a glow-in-the-dark look in dim light (and making cats frustrating subjects of flash photography).

Felines share this characteristic with other crepuscular animals (those that are active primarily at dawn and dusk), but it was a cat that inspired a road safety innovation that has saved many lives. In 1933, Percy Shaw, from Halifax, West Yorkshire, was driving along a dark stretch of road when he saw a pair of green lights. It turned out to be a cat's eyes reflecting in his headlights. Struck by inspiration, Shaw went home and developed a reflective road stud, which he called the Catseye.

Why cats don't need sunglasses

People wear shades to shield their eyes from the glare of the sun, but cats have a superior design feature in their eyes which makes these accessories unnecessary: pupils which contract to a vertical slit. In the wild, cat survival depends on the ability to see as much as possible in dim light. But cats' eyes are also extremely well-adapted to controlling how much light hits the eye in bright sunlight. The vertical slit of the pupil combined with the horizontal line of the eyelids gives the cat maximum control over the light entering the eye.

A nose for it

A cat's sense of smell is roughly fourteen times stronger than ours. They use these superior sniffing skills to make sense of the world around them and, crucially, to locate and catch prey. Cats have a better sense of smell than humans because they have a larger olfactory epithelium – the layer of tissue which sits inside the nose and is involved in odour detection. In cats, this tissue is around 20cm^2. In humans, by contrast, it is a little under 5cm^2. The feline olfactory epithelium is not only much bigger than the human version, it also contains far more scent receptor cells. Cats have around 200 million scent receptors, whereas humans only have a paltry five million or so.

The vomeronasal organ

Cats, along with many other animals (although not humans), have an auxiliary sense organ in the roof of the mouth known as the vomeronasal organ (VNO). This allows them to 'taste' smells and is thought to be particularly useful when it comes to deciphering pheromones (chemicals which affect the behaviour of other members of the same species).

Cat owners will be familiar with the face their cat pulls when taking in scents with their VNO, even if they don't realise exactly what the cat is doing. When cats open their mouths slightly, twitch their noses and appear to grimace, they are actually tasting scent signals in the air. This expression is called the flehman response and it sends interesting olfactory information straight to the VNO. This distinctive gesture is just as common in big cats as it is in our own feline friends.

By a whisker

The cat's whiskers are a remarkable bit of kit that help cats navigate in the dark, detect slight movements and negotiate small openings. Whiskers, also known as *vibrissae*, are much thicker and more deeply rooted than cat hair and they are connected to nerves under the skin. Cats use their whiskers to sense tiny changes in air currents, which helps them avoid obstacles in poor light and detect the movement of prey.

Cats can move their whiskers forward or backward, and whisker position tells us something about how the cat is feeling. When the cat is relaxed the whiskers hang slightly forward, but when a cat feels threatened they are generally drawn back. When a cat is hunting, the whiskers are often forward so they can read as much information about what's going on around them as possible. Cats have a few additional whiskers above their eyes, which trigger a blink response, as well as on the side of the head and near the ankles. All of these combined help cats work out if they'll be able to fit through an opening.

All ears

Cats have a similar hearing range to humans as far as low-frequency sounds go, but high-pitched squeaks and squeals are another matter – this is where cats really excel. Cats can detect sounds around 1.6 octaves higher than humans because they can hear noises at ultrasound frequencies – that is, sounds too high for humans to hear (above about 20kHz). As hunters, cats need to be able to tune in to every creak and rustle that might lead them to a tasty morsel, so acute hearing is an essential skill. Cats are also able to swivel their ears so they can more accurately pinpoint the source of a sound. This sensitivity to high-pitched noises may explain why cats sometimes become a little tetchy if there's a lot of noise in the house and why they don't take kindly to being shouted at.

Scratch that

There can't be a cat owner in the world who hasn't found themselves at the sharp end of the cat's secret weapon: retractable claws. Even the most adorable bundle of kitten fluff comes fully tooled up with deadly talons hidden in its cute little paws. Obviously, these powerful nails are useful for holding on to prey, but they are also very handy when it comes to climbing. Cats have evolved to be brilliant tree-climbers, but clawing their way up curtains is also a lot of fun.

Lots of animals have claws, but very few can tidy them away at will. All cats, big and small, have retractable claws (although the cheetah's are only semi-retractable), as do members of the obscure *viverrid* family, which includes civets. Cats can voluntarily get their claws out on one or more paws at a time, and being able to retract them is useful to prevent getting stuck. Much better to be able to whip them out when they need some traction or want to take a swipe at something. Keeping them tucked away inside a layer of skin and fur also protects them when they're not in use.

Rough and ready

That sandpaper tongue certainly makes being licked by a cat an unusual experience, but that's obviously not its primary purpose. A cat's tongue is covered in tiny, back-to-front hooks, called *papillae*, which are fantastically useful for ripping flesh from bones. The cat's rough tongue is not only useful for devouring prey, it also serves as the perfect self-pampering tool when it acts like a comb for grooming.

Lapping it up

Cats have very different drinking habits to us. They don't slurp, for a start, or even sip, and they're more likely to fight with a straw than use one to suck up cocktails. But they do something with liquid that is completely beyond us: lapping. Some animals (including humans) use some form of suction to get liquid into the mouth, others (such as dogs) use the tongue as a kind of spoon to scoop water in. Cats, however, have a different technique, which has recently been studied in close-up, thanks to high-speed cameras.

Cats, it seems, have a remarkable grasp of physics. When a cat hits the water bowl, they tap into the combined forces of surface tension and gravity to get water into their mouths. The tongue curls backwards and the tip just touches the surface without breaking it. Some liquid attaches to the fast-moving tongue and is drawn upwards into the cat's mouth before falling back into the bowl (pulled down by gravity). Cats need impeccable timing to pull this off; if they lap too slowly, the liquid will just fall off the tongue before it gets into the mouth. It's been observed that cats do about four laps a second (bringing in about 0.1 millilitres of liquid per lap). Explaining how they do this is one thing, but understanding why they bother is another matter. Cats certainly make less mess while drinking than many other animals and perhaps their general cleanliness and dislike of water could explain why they'd rather not splash themselves while they're having a drink.

On balance

Let's be honest, we've all witnessed our cats overshoot a target or take a tumble while making a leap. Yet, despite the occasional misjudged manoeuvre, there's no doubt that cats are nature's acrobats. Their bodies are incredibly supple (ideal for washing those hard-to-reach parts) and they are so agile they can jump five or six times their body height from a standing position. They are also capable of trotting along a narrow garden fence with ease. Cats have remarkably strong muscles in their back legs and highly flexible skeletons. But what really gives them the edge when it comes to their balancing act is something called the vestibular system, which is a group of semi-circular canals in the inner ear. The fluid in these canals moves as the head does, sending signals to the brain about which way is up. Humans and other mammals have a vestibular system too, but cats make much more effective use of theirs. It is this system which enables cats to right themselves if they fall, so they land on their feet. Of course, even cats can make a mistake, and a falling feline can still end up with some nasty injuries, but they're much better equipped than most other animals when it comes to a soft landing.

Landing on your feet

Research by New York veterinarians has revealed some intriguing facts about what happens to cats when they fall out of windows in high-rise apartments. Around 90% of cats studied survived the fall, but cats that fell from nine or more storeys were less likely to be killed and suffered fewer injuries than those who fell shorter distances. Similar studies in other American cities where high-rise living is commonplace have come to the same conclusion. Cats are naturally well-adapted to jumping up and they have also evolved mechanisms to help them should they fall. When a cat falls, they immediately start to re-position the body so their feet are pointing down.

The reason cats who fall from greater heights are more likely to survive and even avoid serious injury may be down to terminal velocity. When an object is dropped from a height, the speed accelerates before reaching terminal velocity, after which it stops accelerating. It's been speculated that it is at this point that a cat spreads out its legs (rather than just extending them downwards) to form a kind of parachute, in the manner of a flying squirrel. This slows down the fall and the cat then lands on all fours. Their flexible frames and supple muscles cushion the impact. It's thought that cats falling from smaller heights may not have enough time for the necessary adjustments. Closing your windows is, of course, a more reliable way of ensuring your cat avoids injury from falling.

Counting toes

A polydactyl might sound a bit like a prehistoric creature, but it is, in fact, any animal with more than the usual number of digits. Cats usually have five toes on each of the front feet and four on the back ones, but some cats suffer from a genetic abnormality, called polydactyly, which usually results in one or two extra toes on the front feet, although the record for the most number of toes on one cat is twenty-eight. Because of the genetic nature of the condition, polydactyl cats tend to cluster – they are most common on the East Coast of North America, and it's thought they may have been taken there as ship's cats from Great Britain. The condition does not generally disadvantage the cat.

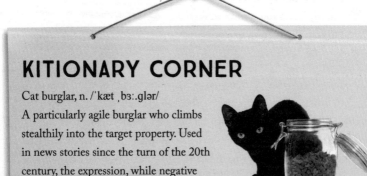

KITIONARY CORNER

Cat burglar, n. /ˈkæt ˌbɜː.glər/
A particularly agile burglar who climbs stealthily into the target property. Used in news stories since the turn of the 20th century, the expression, while negative when applied to humans, conveys a sneaking admiration for the physical prowess of cats.

A tight squeeze

Pity the human gymnast, restricted as they are by a fixed collarbone. The cat, by contrast, has no such limitations. Cats have what is known as a free-floating clavicle, which allows for greater flexibility and makes it possible for cats to turn in mid-air as well as squeeze through tiny spaces.

Treetop felines

Cats are expert athletes and skilled climbers, so why do humans always think they can't get down from that tree? Most of the time, cats that look as if they're in a tight spot – in a tree, on a roof, or some other place not readily accessible to humans – will come down of their own accord eventually. In fact, trying to retrieve the cat yourself might make matters worse, as the cat may become stressed and climb further up, so unless the cat is obviously injured or in imminent danger, it's probably best to watch and wait for a while. Cats sometimes climb down trees backwards, using their claws to grip the bark. This may look a little undignified, but it's actually a safe and controlled way for a cat to come back down to earth.

Ten fascinating facts about the feline form

All felines are obligate carnivores, which means that (unlike many other meat eaters) they cannot survive on a vegetarian diet.

Cats usually have twenty-four whiskers which are arranged in four rows of three on either side of the face.

Over 99.96% of tortoiseshell cats are female because two X chromosomes are needed to pass on this attractive colouration.

On average, a cat's skeleton contains around 230-240 bones (humans have 206), and 10% of the bones are in the tail.

Cats have a preference for using either the left paw or the right one, with females much more likely to be 'right-pawed' than males.

Cats can run up to 30 mph (nearly as fast as a tiger), but they can only sustain this speed for short bursts.

Cats have 32 muscles in each ear and they can rotate each one independently to a full 180 degrees to pinpoint the direction of sounds.

Molar teeth in cats lack flat, grinding surfaces, so they swallow chunks whole rather than chewing. Their front incisors are mainly used for grooming.

Cats regularly shed the outer layer of their claws when the claw outgrows the blood supply, revealing a sharper new claw underneath.

Ovulation in female cats doesn't occur until after mating and is triggered by the sharp spines on a tomcat's penis.

Paternity test

Female cats don't ovulate until one or two days after their first mating, which means the first tom is not usually the father. The female (or queen) will then mate with a number of toms over the following week or so. The result of this often very noisy and usually nocturnal activity can be one litter, many fathers. It's perfectly possible for every kitten in a litter to have a different father, which is why you sometimes get litter-mates who differ in looks and temperament. Cats are extremely prolific breeders – left unneutered, a female cat can be responsible for around 20,000 kittens in five years.

KITIONARY CORNER

Queen, n. /kwiːn/

Queen (originally queen-cat) has been used since the 1670s to describe a female cat capable of breeding. Female cats have also been known as doe-cats.

Rat trap

All parasites need a host, and cats are the unwitting carrier of choice for the *toxoplasma gondii* parasite, which causes an infection called toxoplasmosis. The parasite can also infect humans (indeed, around a third of us will probably be infected with it at some point), although it's usually symptomless. The presence of the parasite rarely causes cats any bother either, but what is truly fascinating about it is the extraordinary way it gets itself transmitted to the host.

Toxoplasma gondii needs to be in a cat's stomach to reproduce, but how does it get in there in the first place? The life cycle of this devious parasite begins in the faeces of an infected cat. If a rat or mouse picks up the parasite, this single-celled organism then travels to the rodent's brain, where it does something remarkable – it interferes with neurons in such a way as to make the rodent apparently fearless in the face of felines. The mind-altering effect of the parasite seems to mimic sexual attraction, drawing the rodent to their unlikely object of desire. Infected rodents have been observed exhibiting behaviour which seems positively suicidal, seeking out cats and throwing themselves into a dance of death at the very claws of their traditional enemy. If the rodent is caught and eaten, the parasite ends up exactly where it wants to be: in the cat's stomach.

CAT BEHAVIOUR

Why our cats do what they do

Cats can be very expressive, both vocally and physically, but despite all the meowing, the purring and the head butts in the shin, we don't always understand exactly what's behind a cat's behaviour. Few owners reflect, for example, on the fact that our cats are rather preoccupied with covering us, our belongings and our property with their scent. Cats spend most of the time sleeping, but are given to bouts of frenetic activity. They do things which annoy us (sitting on a book we're trying to read), or which make us laugh (trying to snuggle up in a slipper), and still more things which just baffle us (bum in the face, anyone?). But whatever they're doing makes perfect sense through a cat's eyes.

Categorically speaking

We don't usually think of cats as particularly noisy (not compared to dogs at any rate), but they can be extremely vocal. Cats produce an astonishing range of sounds, from plaintiff meows to tigerish growls, with a whole load of chattering, chirruping, hissing, howling and caterwauling in between. Scientists have noted nineteen different vocal patterns in cats and it's common for cats to add their own personal sounds to the list, making them one of the most talkative animals around.

Given that domestic cats are descended from largely solitary wildcats, it's not immediately apparent why they should have developed such a complex system of vocal communication. Females do use a range of sounds to communicate with their kittens, but wildcats rarely meow as a way of communicating with other adult cats. In fact, the purpose of the meow in the wild is not fully understood. Tellingly, feral cats – despite being every bit as domestic as our pets – are also much less vocal.

It seems likely, then, that these chatty tendencies have developed and expanded as a direct result of close association with humans. So, yes, your cat really is trying to tell you something. Humans are hard-wired to respond to vocalisations (this is why babies make so much noise well before they have anything interesting to say for themselves) and cats have learnt that 'speaking' to us is often rewarded with attention or food. With a bit of practice, humans can even be taught to follow instructions. 'Feed me', 'let me out', 'let me in again' are orders that most humans can be trained to understand.

It's not just the meow that can be used to control human behaviour. Cats cunningly use their purrs to encourage us to satisfy their every whim. Scientists have recorded two distinct types of cat purr. The non-solicitation purr expresses general contentment and is often heard when a cat is being stroked. The solicitation purr, by contrast, seems to be aimed very squarely at us and is commonly heard when a cat anticipates food. This second type of purr is faster and contains peaks of louder, higher frequency sounds (similar to the frequency of a crying baby). Humans generally find this second purr more annoying, but also hard to ignore. Nothing gets a person running to the cat-food cupboard more quickly than a strategically deployed solicitation purr.

Good vibrations

That soft, soothing purring sound has to be one of the greatest joys of sharing your life with a cat. The word 'purr' generally suggests contentment and satisfaction, whether applied to a cat or a human, but how do cats produce such a beguiling sound and what does it really mean?

Firstly, the technicalities. Cats use their larynx and diaphragm muscles to purr, producing 20–30 vibrations per second, and they're able to do this while both inhaling and exhaling. Domestic cats are not the only purring felines, but cats can either roar or purr – not both. Lions, for instance, can manage a magnificent roar but can't purr for toffee.

Cats purr when they're having a special moment with their owners and they can also purr when they're in contact with other familiar cats they feel bonded to. Cat friends often purr when they are resting together, grooming each other or rubbing against each other. This cat-to-cat purring begins very early – almost as soon as a cat's life begins. Newborn kittens respond to the vibrations of their mother's purring before they can see or hear and they are able to purr back to their mother after a couple of days. Purring keeps mother and kitten in close contact and may also encourage milk flow from the mother. This scene of maternal bliss may seem an obvious explanation as to why purring is associated with contentment, but purring is more than a comfort blanket. Female cats also purr while they are giving birth, a time of considerable exertion. In fact, it's not unusual for cats to purr when they are in pain or distress or even dying. Screaming in pain is likely to attract the attention of enemies, so cats have developed a quieter way to soothe themselves. The purr is not so much an expression of happiness as a self-soothing mechanism which works in good times and bad.

It has even been suggested that the frequency of purr vibrations may actually promote bone healing and tissue repair. The theory goes that purring in cats may have a similar effect to humans doing weight-bearing exercise (which is recommended to maintain healthy bones) and could explain why cats are not especially prone to bone conditions, despite spending so much time doing nothing much at all. This theory has yet to be conclusively validated by scientific evidence so, for now, all we can say is that purring seems to make cats feel better and is much appreciated by cat owners.

KITIONARY CORNER

Purr, v. n. /pə:/

An imitative word to describe the low, vibratory sounds produced by cats, generally thought to be a sign of contentment or pleasure. In use since at least the 1620s, the word has more recently also applied to human expressions of satisfaction.

Tail talk

A cat's tail plays an important role in balancing and can be used as a counterbalance when jumping or making sharp turns. But there's far more to the cat's tail than movement alone – a cat's tail can express mood and intent or act as an invitation or a warning. A cat with its tail stuck up high in the air is confident and content. A cat that's particularly pleased to see you may add a little wiggle. A question mark curve at the end of the tail can indicate a somewhat more cautious interest. A cat with a lowered tail may be feeling defensive or aggressive, while a thrashing tail suggests irritability or agitation. The 'witch's cat' look, with tail fully bristled and erect (often accompanied by an arched back and some hissing), means, as you might expect, 'I'm really annoyed.'

Raising the hackles

Human hair can stand on end when we are cold or experience strong emotions such as anger and fear, but, let's face it, our coats are not much to write home about, so the result is just some little goosebumps, rather than the more impressive display of a cat whose hackles are raised. Fighting is a risky undertaking, so most animals prefer to avoid direct confrontation with an enemy or competitor. One way of achieving this is to make themselves appear much bigger than they really are, so any potential foe is intimidated into backing down. Cats do this magnificently by fluffing out their fur, particularly along the tail and spine. The technical term for this is piloerection and it's an involuntary reaction to stressful situations.

Hooked on catnip

Catnip is an innocent-looking herbaceous plant which belongs to the mint family. It doesn't have much effect on humans (although it has been used as a medicinal herb), but it drives cats wild. Catnip contains a chemical called nepetalactone, which causes cats to roll around in a trance-like state of apparent ecstasy for ten minutes or so. A similar effect has also been observed in big cats. It's not known exactly how catnip works on the feline brain, but it doesn't do cats any harm. Not all cats get to experience this catnip joy – about half of cats don't have a reaction and responsiveness to the plant is thought to be hereditary.

Time for a cat nap

The big advantage of dining on hunks of meat instead of nibbling blades of grass is that you don't have to spend all day doing it. That leaves more time for one of the cat's greatest pleasures – napping. All felines, big and small, spend most of their time sleeping. Domestic cats typically spend around sixteen hours a day asleep (longer for very young and elderly cats). They need to preserve their energy for all that hunting (at least their ancestors did) and it's much more important that they're alert at dawn and dusk than at any other time during the day, as that is when their traditional prey are most active. Cats are often just dozing, rather than in a deep sleep, so they can react instantly should anything untoward occur. Cats will often find somewhere warm, snug and hidden away to sleep, but they can also baffle and amuse their owners by curling up for a snooze in the most unlikely and awkward-looking spots, from shopping bags to shoes to bathroom sinks.

KITIONARY CORNER

Catnap, n. v. /ˈkatnap/

A short sleep taken during the day, often while sitting rather than lying in bed. Recorded since the 1820s, the term reflects the way cats tend to fall asleep wherever they are, but can also become fully alert after only a brief snooze.

Boxing clever

Rather like small children on Christmas day, cats can seem more drawn to the cardboard box their present came in than the present itself. Cats love jumping into the box and then out of it and then back into it again, and are often found sleeping in boxes (even when you've bought them a lovely cat bed). This is probably because cats feel safe when concealed. Cats are not naturally claustrophobic and generally love the feeling of being at least partially enclosed. Research on cats in re-homing shelters suggests that they settle in more easily and exhibit fewer signs of stress if there is a cardboard box in the pen.

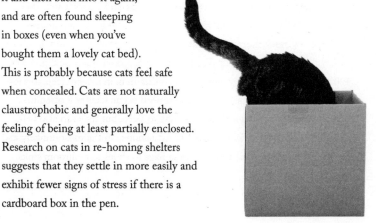

Ten everyday cat acts explained

RUBBING AGAINST YOUR LEGS: Cats aren't just saying hello when they rub against your legs – they are actually marking their territory. Cats have scent glands on their faces and they use these to cover us with the (undetectable to humans) scent of their own pheromones. Once suitably perfumed, we are marked as a safe and familiar part of the cat's universe.

SNIFFING NOSES: When cats greet each other, they often sniff noses. This is another opportunity for scent exchange (this is also why cats will rub against our faces if they can get high enough) and getting up-to-date information about how the other cat is and what they've been up to.

SCRATCHING POSTS (OR THE BACK OF YOUR SOFA): Scratching is an essential behaviour for cats. It keeps the claws in good condition and releases scent from glands in the cat's paws to mark territory and leave important messages to other cats (such as 'Back off, this is my patch').

SPRAYING AROUND THE HOUSE: Generally regarded as the cleanest of animals, some cats – particularly unneutered toms – can develop the unfortunate habit of spraying around the house. This is normal territory-marking behaviour outside, but it usually indicates some form of stress when a cat feels the need to do this in their own home.

BURYING (OR NOT BURYING) POO: Cats tend to do their 'business' somewhere private and then cover it over with earth or litter. Sometimes, however, cats do something called middening, which is when they deliberately leave their faeces exposed (just outside a litter tray, for example) as a way of asserting their claim to a territory.

KNEADING ON YOUR LAP OR A PILLOW: This familiar behaviour is often accompanied by loud and furious purring and may involve sharp claws. It's not entirely clear why adult cats do this, but kittens knead when they feed from their mothers and it may be a reassuring habit they retain into adulthood.

STICKING THEIR BUM IN YOUR FACE: A bum in the face is actually a friendly gesture when it comes from a cat. They are allowing themselves to be in a vulnerable position because they trust you and think you might want to have a sniff by way of saying hello. Think of it as a kitty handshake.

SITTING ON YOUR COMPUTER: Electronic equipment seems to have a special attraction for cats. Gadgets are often warm, which explains part of the appeal, but they also command a lot of your attention. Cats who try to sit on your computer while you're working (or sit on your book or newspaper) are probably just after some fuss.

FASTIDIOUS GROOMING: Cats may spend as much as a third of their waking hours washing themselves. A cat's sandpaper tongue not only washes the fur, but also removes dead hair, skin and any other debris. Grooming also releases oils which keep the coat weatherproof and may help with temperature regulation.

HAVING A 'MAD HALF-HOUR': Cats can sometimes turn into demons possessed and suddenly start zipping about in a frenzy for no apparent reason before, just as suddenly, curling up quietly again. The life of a cat in the wild is one of hours of idleness punctuated by brief but frenetic periods of roaming and hunting. The mad half-hour is just the way our more pampered domestic cats let off a bit of steam.

Food, glorious food

Cats are notoriously picky eaters and many owners have experienced the frustration of trying to find just the thing that their cats will enjoy. Some cats will happily eat one particular food for a while and then seem to go off it completely. Some cats will only eat biscuits, some will only eat chunks in gravy, while others won't touch the stuff. In the wild, cats eat little and often and always something that's fresh (and never, obviously, straight out of the fridge). This goes some way to explaining why cats often like a varied diet, don't always finish their food and won't eat something that's too cold or has been hanging about for a while. Cats may also go off their food if they are ill, distressed or don't feel safe around their feeding area.

Cats can even be finickity about the water they drink. They should always be supplied with fresh water, but they may on occasion turn their noses up at the perfectly clean water in their perfectly clean bowl, preferring instead the water in a puddle. They are also often fond of drinking from a dripping tap or lapping from the glass of water you've left beside your bed.

It goes without saying that, in the wild, a cat's water would never taste of chlorine (unlike our treated water, presented to them in our chemically cleaned bowls) and they would naturally drink from moving water (rivers, streams and so on). In fact, cats – descended as they are from desert animals – don't actually need that much water (although they will need more if they are on a dry-food diet), but they do like a water source that is not right next to their food (the idea of water contaminated by food doesn't appeal).

The cat that got the cream

The idea that cats go wild for milk (or, better still, cream) is firmly fixed in the public's imagination. The fact is, however, most adult cats don't have the right sort of enzymes to digest milk. Kittens are born with an enzyme, lactase, which enables them to absorb the vital nutrients in their mother's milk, but as they grow up this disappears from their stomachs, making them lactose-intolerant. Milk can give adult cats an upset stomach and is best avoided.

Would you like some wool with your meal?

Some cats are drawn to eating inedible items, most commonly wool and other fabrics. Certain pedigree breeds, notably Siamese and Burmese, are particularly prone to this condition, which is known as pica. It's not fully understood why some cats do this, but it's thought that the act of chewing these materials generates pleasure in certain cats that are genetically predisposed to the condition, which then becomes a form of addiction. This potentially dangerous behaviour is hard to explain and difficult to treat, but should be discouraged because it can lead to serious obstructions in the digestive tract.

THE CAT'S MIND

What makes our cats tick?

Even the most devoted cat person has to admit that cats can sometimes seem unfathomable, contrary creatures. They are independent and like to be alone, yet sometimes they yowl for company and cling to laps. They are free-spirited adventurers who also love home comforts. Their moods can be unpredictable and they have a tendency to switch from 'love me' to 'leave me' in a nanosecond. They sometimes bite (or scratch) the hand that feeds them and seem to be drawn to people who don't even like cats. Understanding what motivates our cats can go a long way to demystifying their behaviour and make our friendship stronger.

Home sweet home

Wildcats really don't like people. In fact, one of the reasons they can be very hard to study is that they tend to scarper at the first whiff of a conservationist. They are, on the other hand, extremely attached to their patch, which they jealously patrol, marking it with scent spray to warn others away. Cats, then, are naturally both territorial and solitary – they love their homes and they love their own company. So where do we fit in? Are we just there to pay the bills for our cat's des res, or do they really care about us?

Researchers have put cats through the Strange Situation Test in a bid to find out. The test was originally developed to measure the attachment small children have to their caregivers and has subsequently also been tried out on dogs. The experiment involves putting the child (or dog) in an unfamiliar room and observing how they react when the caregiver is present and absent, and when a stranger is in the room. Dogs, like children, tend to look to their caregiver for reassurance and appear to be upset when the caregiver leaves. This reaction suggests a secure attachment between child and parent, or dog and owner. When the experiment was carried out on cats, however, the cats weren't that bothered whether their owner was there or not. They neither turned to the owner for guidance nor showed signs of concern when the owner left.

This is not, of course, surprising. Put into an unfamiliar space, the first thing a cat will want to do is make sure the area is safe. In the wild, they wouldn't have anyone else to count on, and they're certainly not going to trust a human to do such an important job. This does not, by any means, prove that cats don't have any attachment at all to their owners. On the contrary, when in the safety of their home territory, cats often actively seek out their owners. They may not need us, but they do choose to be in our company when it's on their terms. This self-reliance also means cats are much less likely to suffer from separation anxiety than dogs and are generally more than content for you to go off to work for the day while they mind the house.

In, out and shake it all about

One cat habit that can test the patience of even the most doting owner is when they ask to be let out of the room and then ask to come back in again just a few moments later. It can seem as if the cat is simply being contrary, but it's just that cats and humans recognise different boundaries. For a human, the living room is the living room and the kitchen is a different space altogether. The garden, of course, belongs to another realm, known as 'outside'. Cats see things differently. The whole house and the area around it is one continuous territory and they like to be able to patrol it unimpeded by unnecessary barriers such as doors. Your cat is not being indecisive about whether to sit in the living room or stay in the kitchen, they are just demanding their rightful access-all-areas privileges.

Turf wars

As naturally solitary animals, cats are instinctively disinclined to share, particularly when it comes to their precious personal space. Modern cats, however, often live in urban areas with a high feline population and have to learn to rub along with other cats. Once again, though, their evolutionary heritage holds them back in this regard. Unlike more social animals, cats have not evolved particularly effective strategies for conflict resolution. At the first sign of trouble, their preferred options are to flee or to hide. Failing that, a full-on fight may be necessary. It has to be said, cats haven't really got the hang of backing down gracefully.

Most pet cats who are allowed outdoors try hard to preserve their own territory. They also usually have a home range which goes beyond their personal patch and will probably overlap with the range of other cats. In a bid to keep the peace, neighbourhood cats often develop a kind of shift system; one cat may sit at the window keeping watch, while the cat across the road has their turn to patrol the block. If a bolder cat refuses to play by the rules, however, the system can break down, leading to all sorts of friction. Cats may launch incursions into enemy territory, or even waltz into another cat's home via the cat flap and steal any available cat food.

In the worst-case scenario, these multiple feline comings and goings can cause significant anxiety and stress. This, in turn, can lead to problem behaviour, such as spraying in the house, food anxiety and destructiveness. Cats have a strong roaming instinct and there's not much owners can do to smooth relations between cats while they're outside, but creating as safe a space as possible within the home can go a long way to ensuring our cats have a place to call their own.

Share and share alike

Many people share their homes with two or more cats perfectly harmoniously. Some cats form strong friendships and are content in each other's company. They may curl up together and happily eat out of the same bowls. Many cats, however, really struggle with communal living. Cats, it turns out, don't like cats as much as cat lovers do and in many cases would rather have the place to themselves. Despite being lone rangers by inclination, cats can form social groups (this behaviour is often observed in feral populations), but rival groups can also form in multi-cat homes and the balance of power between cliques or individuals may shift over time.

Just because the cats aren't hissing at each other and fighting all the time, doesn't mean they are the best of friends. Cats keep their feelings to themselves. Some cats will take it in turns to occupy certain spaces, but other cats can be bullies and will block access to key spaces such as stairways and feeding areas. Providing lots of safe areas for all the cats can go a long way to easing tensions, but, in the end, if one cat really can't make a go of it in the group, they may vote with their paws and move out.

Fighting like cats and dogs

If cartoons were your only source of information about the world you'd be convinced that cats and dogs are sworn enemies, destined to a perpetual scrap. Happily, however, cats and dogs can and do live together happily, although there's no denying that the fur sometimes flies when our two favourite domestic animals encounter each other. Despite the Tom and Jerry model (where the cat is the main culprit in any conflict and the dog is, rather unrealistically, on the side of the mouse), it is the cat who is most likely to suffer when cat and dog encounters go badly.

It's not that dogs hate cats; in fact, they often like them very much indeed. It's just that cats rarely enjoy the attentions of an overexcited canine. Cats and dogs have very different instincts and motivations and they're not able to read books which could give them handy tips on how to get along together. Cats can be extremely stressed by the very presence of a dog. Imagine being stuck in a cat basket at the vet and some slobbering, drooling idiot of a beast sticks its nose in at you. The fact that its owner assures your owner that the canine in question loves cats is hardly likely to reduce your blood pressure.

Some dogs are less annoying than others, from a cat's point of view, depending on breed and individual temperament, and there are dogs that show respect to their feline friends. Dogs that are raised with cats from puppies are more likely to be able to keep their cool around them, but the way a cat moves does tend to trigger even the nicest dog's chase instinct, which is never a pleasant experience for a cat.

KITIONARY CORNER

Cat fight, n. v. /kætfaɪt/

First used to describe an altercation between cats in *The Cat Fight*, a mock-heroic poem published in 1824, usage was extended to refer to squabbling women a few decades later. A cat fight usually involves low-level violence,  including scratching and hair-pulling, but may also be verbal rather than physical.

Is that budgie for me?

While cats are most likely to be the wronged party when it comes to feline-canine relationships, the same definitely can't be said when it comes to other species commonly kept as pets (although tortoises probably have little to fear). Cats are natural-born killers of birds and rodents, and you wouldn't bet money on the rabbit in a cat versus bunny contest. Nevertheless, some people do manage households which include numerous species. A cheeky budgerigar sat on a cat's head, or a kitten adorably snuggling a bunny are meat and drink to the greetings-card industry and such images are often found on the internet. But small animals have an inherent fear of their natural predators and tend to freeze rather than fight if they're in a tight spot. Just because they're not squawking or squealing, doesn't mean they're not terrified.

Perverse affections

Cats often seem drawn to people who don't like them. When a cat enters a room they have a knack of selecting the lap of the one person who's a bit afraid of cats, while sauntering casually past the people who really love them. This is particularly bad news for ailurophobes (people who suffer from an irrational fear of cats) and may seem to confirm some people's suspicions that cats are not very nice. But there is a perfectly logical explanation for this seemingly perverse behaviour. Put simply, cats don't like to be stared at (eye contact is seen as a direct and not very friendly challenge in the feline world). Yet, what do animal lovers do when they see an animal? They stare at it. Worse still, the cat lovers in the room may not only be looking directly at the cat, but also waving their hands about and making silly puss-puss noises. The ailurophobe, on the other hand, will be still and silent, doing their best not to attract the cat's attention. Counterintuitively, this avoidance behaviour puts the cat at ease and makes for an inviting lap.

Love me, love me not

The trouble with some humans is that they just don't know when to stop. At least that's how it must seem to cats, who can only take so much fussing and cuddling. Lots of cats do enjoy physical affection from their owners, but lying on a lap or losing yourself in the moment puts you in a vulnerable position and is actually quite unnatural for a cat. This can lead to what is known as the 'petting and biting syndrome', which may come about because a cat is torn between pleasure and their natural instinct for self-preservation. Another situation which may lead to a misunderstanding is if a cat nods off while you're stroking them, only to wake suddenly to find that they're being threatened by a strange creature. They may then launch a counterattack before they realise it's just their owner's hand.

People can find themselves at the wrong end of a tooth or claw because they have misinterpreted a cat's behaviour. The so-called 'social roll' is one typical example. This is when a cat rolls over, stretches out all floppy and relaxed and does a full belly display. This is a friendly gesture, indicating a happy cat content to be in your company, but it is not a request for a belly rub. Generally speaking, cats do not like having their stomach area touched. Attempting to do this may result in hisses and scratches (and some hurt feelings on both sides).

Another mistake we make is assuming our cats need to be comforted. If a cat appears anxious (because a dog is walking past the house, for example), our natural instinct is to offer reassurance, as we would a child. But the cat may be in full wildcat defence mode and any interference from you may just provoke some redirected aggression. Also, don't bother them when they're busy. If your cat is stalking, prowling, patrolling or hunting, probably best to leave them alone. Individual cats vary enormously in how much physical attention they crave or can tolerate, but whatever affection you get from your cat should be appreciated – it's not given lightly.

TEN THINGS YOUR CAT WANTS YOU TO UNDERSTAND

Cats in the wild don't need to express their emotions publicly because they tend to live alone. Indeed, baring their souls might reveal their weaknesses to enemies or competitors and put them in danger. This is why cats can be very hard to read. Humans, as highly social animals, don't always understand what's going on in a cat's head and often miss the subtle signs that may indicate stress. If they were a tad more communicative, these are some of the things our cats would like to say to us:

I don't always feel like being picked up.

I really hate people staring at me.

I'm not being naughty when I scratch stuff.

I can't help being really alert first thing in the morning.

I need access to high places where I can feel safe.

I don't want to eat my dinner next to my litter tray or my water bowl.

I want my litter tray in a quiet area and cleaned every day.

I want to have the choice to come to you.

I like my cat carrier covered with a blanket to help me feel safe.

I need a hiding place where I know I'll be left alone.

Thanks, you really shouldn't have

Everybody knows that cats are predatory hunters, yet when they shoot through the cat flap with a live mouse in their jaws, it can still provoke shock, surprise and horror. Some people are troubled by the way a cat appears to toy with its catch. It can be an uncomfortable spectacle, but cats don't do this because they are cruel. Pet cats obviously don't need to hunt in order to survive, but domestic cats remain little changed since their wild days and the drive to hunt is still very much with them.

When a well-fed cat does catch something, it is surplus to requirements, so they don't feel the need to eat it straightaway (feral cats are much less likely to play with their prey in this way). This is probably one of the reasons why cats frequently bring their prey home, although people often think they're being given a 'gift' (however unwelcome). There is some debate as to why cats do this. One explanation is that cats are so horrified by our poor hunting skills, they think they need to show us how it's done. Another theory is that cats regard us as big kittens and they're just bringing us our dinner. The problem with these ideas, though, is that they assume cats feel responsible for feeding us (which seems unlikely) and that they can't tell the difference between people and cats (which also seems unlikely). More plausible is that the cat doesn't really need a dead mouse right now, so they'll leave it lying at the bottom of the stairs in case they need it later.

Too cool for school?

Dogs, so the adage goes, have masters; cats have staff. This sentiment reflects the widely held belief that cats are disinclined to follow orders and are not overly motivated by a desire to please their owners. While dog owners trot along to puppy-obedience classes, training is not something most cat owners ever think about at all. Maybe it's time for a rethink. Cats, after all, are intelligent animals and many of them do enjoy interacting with their owners.

Cats can respond to positive, reward-based training and a growing number of behaviourists are recommending that we put a bit more effort into making sure our cats get a good education. In the first place, a little bit of training can make life easier when it comes to everyday practicalities, such as getting a cat into a carrier or standing still for a groom or a vet check. If you want to go further, cats can also be trained to perform basic tricks, such as begging, sitting or even fetching things. Cats may enjoy learning how to jump through hoops, into boxes or onto chairs, which is a good way of providing them with both physical exercise and mental stimulation. Training cats does require a bit of patience, and short sessions are best, with lots of tasty rewards. Just because cats are independent-minded, doesn't mean they can't learn new tricks.

WHO'S YOUR FATHER?

Encounters with pedigree cats

Cats have never been subject to the kind of selective breeding which has given us dogs of all shapes and sizes. They are naturally highly adept at pest control, so there's been no call for human intervention to create a superior mouser. Cats don't really have the work ethic for any other occupation, so people haven't felt much need to interfere with feline reproduction. Consequently, the vast majority of pet cats in the world today came into existence without any meddling from humans. Nevertheless, a number of pedigree breeds have been developed by enthusiasts over the last century or so, and just under ten percent of pet cats in the UK are pedigrees. New breeds, or varieties of existing breeds, are being developed and recognised all the time, especially in the United States.

What is a pedigree cat?

Put simply, a pedigree cat is one which belongs to a recognised breed. A pedigree may be registered with a national or international cat organisation and may have documentation detailing a pedigree going back several generations. There are around fifty recognised cat breeds (depending on who's counting). Some of them are long-established and well-known, such as the Siamese or the Russian Blue, and some are much more recent creations, such as the Toyger, a striped breed developed in the 1980s.

The differences between one pedigree cat breed and another are nowhere near as stark as the variations commonly found among pedigree dogs. Pedigree cats may vary in size (although you won't find anything like the extremes of Yorkshire Terriers and Irish Wolfhounds), but the basic anatomical structure of all cats is more or less the same, apart from a number of short-faced breeds, such as the Persian. Most of the differences between cat breeds are down to relatively superficial factors such as coat type, pattern and colour.

TEN CLASSIC CAT BREEDS

Some of these pedigree breeds were recognised in the very early days of the organised cat show and they all claim a history which goes much further back. But just because today's version of the breed may look a lot like cats described in times long gone, doesn't mean there really is an unbroken line of descent. Cats have generally been left to choose their own partners and nobody much bothered with controlled breeding until recent times. Any cat has the right to claim an ancient heritage, but even the proudest pedigree cat almost certainly has a long line of moggies somewhere in their family tree.

Siamese: Once associated with the royal family of Siam (now Thailand), this is one of the most popular and best-known pedigree breeds. There are drawings of Siamese cats in a book called *Tamra Maew* (which means 'cat poems'), which dates back to the 14th century. Known for their tendency to 'talk', Siamese cats are extremely sociable and love company.

Burmese: This seemingly ancient cat is said to have been valued as a sacred animal in the ancient temples of Burma. They appeared at early cat shows in Britain, but were overshadowed by the much more popular Siamese, which they resemble. Most modern Burmese cats are thought to be descended from a single female, called Wong Mau, imported into America in the 1930s and bred with a Siamese.

Abyssinian: This breed takes its name from the ancient empire of Abyssinia (now Ethiopia), which is in the region where the earliest domestic cats are known to have lived. It's thought that soldiers serving in North Africa during the 19th century may have brought cats home with them to Britain, where the breed was developed.

Persian: One of the most familiar pedigree cats, this long-coated glamour puss originated in Persia (now Iran) and was first seen in Europe when some were imported into Italy in the 1600s. The breed's high-maintenance coat comes in a wide range of colours and its distinctive flat face has become more exaggerated over generations of selective breeding.

Turkish Angora: This long-haired cat shares its name and its silky coat with the goats and rabbits that are also native to the Angora region of Turkey (now known as Ankara). Probably first imported into Western Europe in the 17th century, these attractive cats commanded high prices in the early days of the cat show.

Russian Blue: This dazzlingly silver-blue cat is said to have arrived in Europe from Russia as a ship's cat in the 19th century. It has, however, been known by a variety of names, suggesting alternative origins, including the Maltese Blue and the Spanish Blue. With a tendency to be shy and sensitive, Russian Blues are nevertheless loyal to their owners.

Chartreux: This French breed claims a heritage dating back to the Middle Ages and is a distinctive blue colour, similar to the better-known Russian Blue. Accounts of blue cats in France emerged in the 16th century, but it

wasn't until after the First World War that concerted efforts were made to fix the Chartreux as a recognised breed.

Norwegian Forest Cat: Sometimes known as the Viking cat, this large, thick-coated breed is well-adapted to a cold climate and is attached to a number of Norse folktales. Probably originating as a farm cat, the breed was recognised by the Norwegian Cat Society in 1912. With an athletic build, the Norwegian Forest cat can be something of a climber.

Maine Coon: This large, long-haired cat is an American breed and was originally kept to keep down rodents. It gets its name from its place of origin and its brush-like tail, which resembles a raccoon's. The Maine Coon is hardy but gentle and is known for the chirping sound it makes. They are intelligent and can be trained to fetch.

British Shorthair: It's

sometimes claimed that the British
Shorthair has a noble heritage going all
the way back to the Romans, which is
true only in as much as nearly all cats in
Britain are descendants of cats introduced
by the Romans. Selective breeding for
desirable characteristics (coat type and
colour, for example) only really began in
the 19th century, so, for all their rosettes,
British Shorthairs are no more or less
ancient than any other British cat with short hair.

Pedigree cats at Battersea

The vast majority of cats coming through the doors at Battersea Dogs &
Cats Home are, of course, moggies. Nevertheless, a handful of pedigree cats
do find themselves in our care. In 2015 there were 39 Bengals, 1 Balinese,
4 Birmans, 2 British Blues, 10 Burmese, 2 Chinchillas, 2 Cornish Rex, 1
Egyptian Mau, 2 Himalayans, 9 Maine Coons, 12 Persians, 6 Ragdolls, 4
Russian Blues, 1 Scottish Fold, 19 Siamese, 1 Sphynx and 1 Tonkinese, and
even a Korat. All were given the same care and dedication as all the other
cats and were rehomed.

Cairo

Penfold

The first fancy felines on the catwalk

Humans love a competition, and domesticated animals have not escaped our fondness for categorising, comparing and selecting the best from the rest. Country fairs and agricultural shows have long been an opportunity to show off prize beef cattle, top egg-layers and the best wool-producers. But most domestic animals are closely controlled, their reproduction carefully managed.

Cats, on the other hand, have been largely left to their own devices when it comes to choosing a mate, despite the fact that they became domesticated thousands of years ago. If a cat has a beautiful coat, a cheerful disposition or exceptional rat-catching skills, it's not generally down to careful husbandry – it's just an accident of nature and not something a human can readily take credit for. Yet still, cat shows exist.

The earliest dog shows divided dogs according to function, and that is still the underlying principle behind the modern canine beauty parade. There are gundogs and herding dogs, dogs that do other jobs and dogs that do nothing other than please people. The categories for competition are based on original purpose rather than pure physique. When it comes to cats, however, you wouldn't have much of a show if they were all just entered into a 'mouser' class. This was the difficulty facing the early proponents of the organised cat show.

One man is credited with being the 'father of the cat fancy' – an illustrator and author called Harrison Weir. He had an interest in natural history and bred pigeons and poultry, as well as cats. He was also keen to establish a taxonomy of cats and a set of standards by which they could be judged. Weir developed 'Points of Excellence', which were the first standards by which cats were judged in the UK. The different features of the cat were awarded points according to their importance – a total of 100 points could be awarded to the 'perfect cat' – and this system of allocating points to cats in cat shows is still widely used today.

It was at Weir's instigation that the first major cat show was held at London's Crystal Palace in 1871. He hoped that by displaying cats to the public in this way he could help raise the status of cats and improve the way they were treated. Here, 170 cats were entered, including Weir's own fourteen-year-old tabby, The Old Lady. The classes were divided according to colour, coat length, shape and build, rather than anything we would recognise as distinct breeds today. The competitors included some of the first Siamese cats to be seen in the UK, as well as Manx cats and even a Scottish wildcat, which won a prize despite its understandably unruly behaviour. The show was an unexpected success with the public and more cat shows quickly followed all over the country. There were classes for 'Short-haired Unusual Colour She-Cats', 'Persian Rare Colour Cats' and 'Wild or Hybrid between Wild and Domestic Cats' – which one year was won by an ocelot (a South American dwarf leopard, which probably didn't want to be carted about in a cat carrier).

Harrison Weir went on to become president of the National Cat Club, founded in 1887, which regulated cat breeding and cat shows. The Governing Council of the Cat Fancy is now the UK's main cat registry organisation and oversees major championship cat shows, as well as setting breed standards. Cats are still judged according to historical origin, coat type

KITIONARY CORNER

Moggy, n. /ˈmɒgi/

'Moggy' has been used to refer specifically to a non-pedigree cat or, more generally, to a perfectly ordinary cat since around 1910. Initially a variant on the woman's name Maggie (from Margaret), a name which was given to cows from the 18th century and was also used to describe a scruffy woman.

and colour, and the modern cat show has a bewildering array of classes, from Oriental Cinnamon and Lilac Point Siamese to Semi-Longhair Aristocrat and British Ticked Tabby.

End of the tail

The Isle of Man is perhaps best known for its high-octane TT motorcycle races, but the island's native feline also gets a look-in on souvenir postcards and fridge magnets. The Manx cat's most distinctive feature is, of course, its missing tail, the result of a naturally occurring genetic mutation which was replicated through an isolated population.

Legends provide more fanciful explanations. One story goes that the Manx was late for the sailing of Noah's Ark and had its tail cut off by the closing doors. Another has it that the Manx is the result of crosses between cats and rabbits (not quite as ridiculous as it may sound, given that Manx cats often have an unusual hopping gait). Still other tales blame Irish or Viking invaders, who were said to prize cats' tails as lucky charms. In order to protect their kittens, so it is said, mother cats bit off their tails. There are also tales of taxes imposed on cats' tails by feudal lords, and shipwrecked tailless cats who had journeyed from as far away as the Far East.

The Isle of Man is clearly not short on folklore, but the Manx cat, in fact, suffers from a genetic disorder related to spina bifida, which affects the spinal column as well as the tail. Not all Manx cats are tailless (rumpies); some have a few vertebrae (stumpies) and some will be born with normal-length tails (longies). Manx cats can have a mixed litter of kittens with full tails, partial tails or no tails at all, but if two cats with the tailless gene are bred together, their kittens are generally miscarried.

Despite this apparently huge genetic disadvantage, the Manx cat has survived over many centuries and still occurs naturally among free-breeding cats on the island. The Manx has been a recognised pedigree breed since the early days of organised cat clubs and they were exhibited at the Crystal Palace Cat Show in 1871.

The remarkable Turkish swimming cat

The elegant, long-haired Turkish Van cat comes from the region around Lake Van in eastern Turkey. Pedigree Vans are generally pure white apart from a splash of colour on the head and tail, although the cats that actually live in Turkey are often just white. The local cats often do share, however, the show variety's long, silky coat, which is well-adapted to both freezing winters and sweltering summers. The breed is said to have a fondness for and even a fascination with water, not a characteristic normally associated with cats, but perhaps not so inexplicable in the hot summers of the Middle East.

The Turkish Van is often credited with an ancient lineage, but it didn't attract the attention of outsiders until the 1950s, when two British journalists, working for the Turkish Tourist Board, were given two kittens. The pair took the cats with them on their travels before eventually returning to the UK. After a spell in quarantine, the two cats became part of the foundation stock for a new pedigree breed, which was officially recognised in 1969.

Where did I leave my coat?

If you want a cat that grabs attention, you couldn't do much better than a Sphynx. Sometimes known as the 'birthday suit cat', this pedigree lacks something which is widely regarded as pretty essential in a feline: fur. The sight of this alien-like creature does tend to set many people on edge, but the hairless Sphynx cat is not without its fans.

The breed came about when a hairless cat was born into a litter of kittens in Canada, back in the 1960s. The kitten was called Prune. If the idea of a cat with no hair makes you uncomfortable, the next part of the story may make you feel even worse. When he grew up, Prune was mated with his mother as part of an attempt (successful, as it turned out) to start a serious breeding programme for hairless cats. Since then the Sphynx has become a recognised pedigree breed, with a small but devoted following.

In whose best interest?

Cats are already amazing creatures, but humans love to meddle with things, including cat genetics, and the result is a range of pedigree breeds with different characteristics. Often these differences are largely superficial – a matter of lilac points or seal ones, say – which are unlikely to have any impact on the cat's enjoyment of life, but the outcome of playing with nature is not always so benign. While breeding for one or two specific features, there is a risk that unanticipated, harmful recessive mutations may emerge. These may go on to cause hereditary diseases, which will inevitably affect the cat's welfare.

When certain exaggerated features become desirable, physical health problems can result. Short noses, for example, with reduced-sized nostrils, can lead to breathing difficulties. Watery eyes are also common in flat-faced cats due to blocked tear ducts. Constant inbreeding also reduces the size of the gene pool over successive generations, causing a lack of 'hybrid vigour', reducing the cat's natural ability to fight infection and disease.

KITIONARY CORNER

Tabby, n. adj. /ˈtabi/
The word 'tabby' comes from the Arabic place name al Attabiyya, which was a district of Baghdad famous from the 12th century for the manufacture of colourful fabrics, particularly striped taffeta. The word travelled through many languages over the centuries, before arriving in England, first to describe fabric and, by the end of the 17th century, to mean a striped cat.

One short step too far?

One breed of cat has stirred up more controversy than perhaps any other. The Munchkin has extremely short legs for a cat and came about as a random and entirely natural mutation. These things happen – but would you really want to turn an unusual genetic event into a recognised pedigree cat breed? This is what one cat owner from Louisiana in the US decided to do when she adopted a litter of short-legged kittens in the 1980s.

The Munchkin has a gene similar to the one that has given the canine world the Corgi and Dachshund (indeed, it is sometimes called the Dachshund cat). But while many people are reasonably untroubled by the fact that dogs are a highly diverse bunch, the general consensus is that cats should be, well, cat-shaped.

Although this striking new breed has been accepted by some cat show organisations, notably in America, others – including Britain's Governing Council of the Cat Fancy – have refused to recognise the Munchkin on the grounds that deliberately breeding for abnormalities is not a positive step and should be discouraged.

TEN MODERN CAT BREEDS

The 'cat fancy' (as the hobby of selective breeding and the showing of cats is often called) was slow to get off the ground compared to similar endeavours for dogs and has a much lower public profile. The hobby has, however, been gathering pace in recent years and aficionados are busy developing new breeds which are gaining recognition by cat show organisations, if not quite yet by the wider public. Here are a few of the new breeds on the block.

Cornish Rex: This cat has an unusual wavy coat and curly whiskers and eyebrows, and is the result of a naturally occurring mutation which appeared in Cornwall in the 1950s. Not long after, a similar mutation popped up in neighbouring Devon, which led to the Devon Rex. The Rex is an affectionate and playful cat that enjoys games and human contact.

Scottish Fold: This controversial breed has a genetic mutation which causes the ears to fold forward. First identified in the 1960s, efforts to establish the breed in cat fancy circles faced severe criticism when

it emerged that the mutation which leads to the distinctive ear folds is also linked to crippling skeletal abnormalities. The Scottish Fold is still a sought-after breed, despite serious concerns about its health.

Ragdoll: Developed in the 1960s, this American breed has a long, silky coat and blue eyes and gets its name from its tendency to become relaxed and floppy when picked up. The Ragdoll has been the subject of a certain amount of controversy due to the mistaken belief that its floppiness was down to a low pain threshold.

Snowshoe: This attractive cat is the result of mixes between Siamese and American Shorthair cats and is distinguished by very particular markings, which are not easy to replicate. Developed in the 1960s, the Snowshoe should have the pointed colouring typical in the Siamese, along with white socks on all four paws.

American Wirehair:

This rare and recent breed came about when an American Shorthair was born with an unusually wiry coat in the 1960s. These cats have coarse, coiled or crimped hair, similar to a terrier dog's, which often springs back to the touch. They are still extremely unusual, even in the cat show world.

Bengal: These energetic and often very vocal cats have a beautiful spotted or marbled coat, giving them the appearance of a wild cat – not surprising given that they came about as the result of cross-breeding domestic cats with the Asian leopard cat in the 1980s. Alert and intelligent, Bengals can be highly territorial and are avid roamers and hunters.

Singapura: One of the smallest recognised pedigree breeds, Singapura cats are said to be descended from cats imported from

Singapore into the United States in the 1970s (although the story spun by the original breeders has been subject to question). These pretty, delicate-looking cats have particularly big eyes and come only in a sepia tint.

Pixiebob: This stubby-tailed cat with the appearance of a wild American bobcat is a new breed which is said to have been naturally occurring and possibly the result of a mating with a wild cat. The Pixiebob was accepted as a breed by some American cat shows in the 1990s and was first seen in Britain in 2004.

LaPerm: This is a relative newcomer to the pedigree cat world and has an unusual curly coat which can be traced back to one single cat. The first LaPerm was a female cat (appropriately named Curly) who appeared in a litter of barn cats in Oregon during the 1980s. Curly passed this new, dominant gene down to her offspring and a new breed was quickly established.

Toyger: This very new breed is the result of deliberate attempts to breed a tiny tiger. Developed in the 1980s, the Toyger's original breeder claimed her intention was to create a domestic cat which would discourage people from trying to keep wild cats as pets. The Toyger looks basically like a tabby with particularly pronounced stripes and has received recognition from a number of international cat show organisations.

CATS IN THE GOOD (AND BAD) OLD DAYS

A history of pedestals and persecution

Once cats had decided it might be worth their while to move a little closer to humans, they quickly made an impression on our imaginations – but cat history should probably come with a warning. The way cats have been treated over the centuries can be distressing to anyone who cares about animal welfare. No civilisation has ever been so enchanted with cats as the ancient Egyptians (they even turned them into gods), but even this devotion led to suffering for millions of animals. Cats have been both worshipped and abused, loved and harmed by various cultures which have had confused and contradictory attitudes towards them. At most points in history some cats have been cherished, while at the very same time others were being feared, persecuted or just ignored.

A civilising influence

No museum exhibition on ancient Egyptian civilisation is complete without at least one feline relic. A small cat statue, perhaps, or a cat sketched onto a scrap of papyrus. Better still, a cat mummy. This preoccupation with cats in the world of Egyptology is a reflection of how extraordinarily significant they were to the ancient Egyptians themselves. Although there are few significant finds from the earliest days of the Pharaohs, the Egyptians went cat crazy about the time of the New Kingdom (around 1500 BC) and left behind millions of cat-related artefacts for us to sift through.

Many of the animals depicted in Egyptian art are highly stylised and symbolic and you can't always count on artistic representation to reflect reality. Nevertheless, the cat pops up often enough in scenes of ordinary family life for us to conclude that real, flesh-and-blood domestic cats were valued, as well as the more spiritual, otherworldly felines of myth. Cats are commonly shown sitting under a woman's chair (a dog sometimes takes up position near the man). This is probably partly symbolic (Egyptians were very impressed by feline fertility, which is why the cat is most closely associated with women), but the cats in these pictures are also just pet cats, naturalistically portrayed.

The physical likeness is certainly there, and there's no doubt that your average Egyptian would have run into cats every single day and very probably had one living in or around the home. Egyptians fed cats on bread dipped in milk and scraps of raw fish. In return, these fairly newly domesticated felines would have made themselves very useful. Not only did they protect food supplies from mice and rats, but they also took on scorpions and snakes (even cobras). No doubt this goes some way to explaining why cats had such high status in Egyptian society, a fact not missed by a number of visiting Greek historians, including Herodotus, who noted that when a cat died the household would go into mourning.

Snakes in the frame

Fatal snake bites were a real and present danger to Egyptians. No wonder, then, that they were much impressed by a predator that could catch and kill a serpent. A cat killing a serpent is a common motif in Egyptian art. Often (and this is where the artist departs somewhat from realism) the cat is wielding a knife and usually resembles a wild cat, possibly a cheetah.

The cat goddess

One of the most familiar icons of ancient Egypt is the cat goddess Bastet. She seems to have replaced or merged with an earlier goddess with the head of a lion, called Sekhmet. Whereas Sekhmet was a warrior, Bastet was a nurturer – embodying the virtues of real-life cats with their strong maternal instincts (not to mention their capacity to become pregnant over and over again). Initially represented in the form of a human female with a cat's head, she became more commonly depicted as a domestic cat from around 1000 BC. She was particularly associated with fertility, childbirth and motherhood. Her form was made into amulets for pregnant women (or those who wanted to become pregnant) to carry around.

The cult of Bastet centred around the temple at Bubastis, a town to the north of Cairo. Hundreds of thousands of pilgrims went to visit the temple, particularly during the annual Bastet festival, which was apparently a riotous, drunken affair. Pilgrims made offerings of little bronze cat statues, as well as mummified cats (hundreds of thousands of cat mummies were excavated at the site). As well as these sacrificial cats, large numbers of cats would have lived in the grounds of the temple, looked after by priests with the help of donations from pilgrims.

Hair tonic

The fur and excrement of cats were put to medicinal use in Egyptian prescriptions. One lotion, which was supposed to stop hair going grey, was made using one crucial ingredient – the placenta of a cat.

All wrapped up

Ancient Egyptians believed that all creatures, human or otherwise, could look forward to an afterlife and that mummification was a necessary process to secure safe passage to the next world. Some special individual animals (favoured pets of the royal family, for instance) were mummified and given elaborate burials in their own right, in a similar fashion to humans. Hundreds of thousands of cats were given ritual burial following death from natural causes, but many, many others were deliberately killed so they could be mummified and offered to the gods.

Millions of animal mummies have been excavated from various sites in Egypt, and more are still being discovered. Cats, dogs, ibises, crocodiles, baboons, mongooses and scarab beetles were mummified in staggering numbers. Indeed, animal mummies were produced on an industrial scale in order to satisfy the huge demand from the great crowds of pilgrims who flocked to the most popular temples. The animals were mostly bred and killed specially for the purpose.

It's hard to reconcile these contradictory attitudes to cats from a modern perspective. On the one hand, they were revered and Egyptians would stand round and watch in awe as cats went about their ordinary business as mousers or mothers. On the other hand, there was mass slaughter, which seems horribly cruel. Egyptians did believe the mummified cats would live on elsewhere, but the scale of this waste of life still seems breathtaking.

Dust to dust

The mad scramble to excavate anything and everything in Egypt (preferably before anyone else got their hands on it) began when Napoleon Bonaparte arrived in Egypt in 1798. The Egyptians' obsessive devotion to creating material objects for their gods has left us with enough cat exhibits for virtually every museum on earth to have one, and countless artefacts have made the journey from Egypt to museums across the world. Priceless and irreplaceable historic objects have not always been well cared for, however. Many mummified remains were exported to Europe, only to be ground up and used as fertiliser. All nineteen tonnes of one particular consignment of mummified cats suffered this fate on arrival in the UK – all that remains is a single skull, which is in the British Museum.

On the tiles

It seems likely that cats first made their way to Italy around the 5th century BC, a time when Egypt was a Roman province. Although the expansive Roman Empire was probably in large part responsible for spreading cats across Europe, they were never revered in the same way as they had been in Egypt. Cats were probably kept to control rodents, but they had no particular status. This is perhaps why there is not a great deal of surviving imagery of Roman cats. One striking exception is a mosaic which was found in a house in Pompeii. It shows a very life-like tabby hunting wildfowl and probably originally formed the centrepiece on the floor of a wealthy home.

Seal of disapproval

Pope Gregory IX issued a papal bull in the 1230s which some say set the stage for centuries of suspicion and hostility towards cats. Vox in *Rama* is a warning against the sin of devil worship and gave powers to the papal inquisitors to root out heretics (using torture if necessary). The edict mentions a black cat, which was apparently involved in a satanic ritual.

The devil's playmate, the witch's friend

It's not really a Halloween party unless at least one person is dressed as a witch's cat. In the collective imagination, cats and witches go together like salt and vinegar. Although now regarded with humour, or even affection, this association is a lingering legacy of some very dark times for the cat.

Magical beliefs and Pagan practices were widespread in Europe long after Christianity had secured a firm foothold across the continent. The Church added fear of the devil into the mix. This unfortunate confluence of folk traditions and religious fervour collided head-on with a series of social, economic and sectarian upheavals which resulted in the mass hysteria that we've come to know as the witch-hunts.

A papal bull published by Pope Innocent VIII in 1484 denounced witchcraft as a heresy, unleashing a witch craze which swept across Europe periodically between the 15th and 18th centuries, reaching a peak between 1580 and 1640. Hundreds of thousands of people (mainly, but not exclusively, women) were caught up in the witch-hunts, which also led to the death of countless cats, guilty by association.

One text at the heart of this mood of paranoia was *Malleus Maleficarum* (The Hammer of the Witches), a book written in 1486 by Heinrich Kramer, a German clergyman and inquisitor. The book set out a framework for witch trials and specifically linked cats to witchcraft. Animal familiars were often named in witch trials and cited as evidence of devilish practices. Cats were not the only animals implicated in magical misdeeds. It was believed that the devil could appear in animal form and that witches could transform themselves into various creatures. Many species were mentioned in trials and folktales, including dogs, pigs, crows, hares and toads.

It is impossible to be precise about how many cats were affected by all this (we're not even sure exactly how many humans lost their lives). Obviously, nobody kept a record every time a cat was killed under suspicion of consorting with the devil, and many records of witch trials were destroyed or subsequently lost. Nevertheless, acts of deliberate cruelty towards cats were a fact of life in many parts of Europe for hundreds of years, in part fuelled by superstitious beliefs about their supposed mystical powers. The motif of the witch's cat has seeped so deeply into our shared culture that we still recognise it today, long after real fear of witchcraft has waned.

A cat called Satan

In 1566 the assizes at Chelmsford, Essex, heard the case against four women under the 1563 Act Against Conjurations, Enchantments and Witchcrafts. Elizabeth Francis confessed to having been taught witchcraft by her grandmother, who also gave her a white-spotted cat. The cat was called Satan and was apparently able to talk and perform supernatural tasks in return for some food, a soft bed and a few drops of blood. Satan (who appears as a toad in some parts of the confession) was also able and willing to cause death. The cat was passed on to one Agnes Waterhouse (apparently in return for some cake). Agnes later found herself charged with 'bewitching to death' (which she denied) as well as killing her neighbour's geese. She became the first woman to be executed for witchcraft in England.

A plague on all your houses

When the Great Plague broke out in London in 1655, there were fears that this deadly pestilence was spread by cats and dogs. Consequently, tens of thousands of cats and dogs were deliberately destroyed. As there is no evidence that cats and dogs were in any way responsible for spreading the disease (fleas transported by rats may have been the culprits, although even this theory has not been proved conclusively), this mass cull did nothing to protect people and something like between 75,000 and 100,000 Londoners lost their lives in what was to be the last of a series of plague epidemics to hit the capital.

Sent to the tower

The Belgian town of Ieper (better known by its French name, Ypres) is most famous in the English speaking world for its First World War battles. It does, however, have another claim to fame – a regular cat parade, called Kattenstoet. The festival has been running since 1955 and is a fun celebration of all things feline. Locals dress up as cats or as figures from key moments in cat history. Witches are a popular theme, as are Egyptians and famous cat characters from Puss in Boots to Garfield.

The focal point of the event is the Cloth Hall and the parade ends with some cats being thrown from the belfry to the town square below. These days, the cats are only toys, but Kattenstoet is a reminder of how cruelly mistreated cats once were. Ypres was at the heart of the textile industry in the Middle Ages and wool was imported from England and stored in the Cloth Hall, which was one of the largest commercial buildings in Europe when it was originally built in the 13th century. This valuable cloth was easily damaged by gnawing rodents, making cats very useful indeed.

All the more inexplicable, then, is that the town has a long history of throwing cats from the tower. Records of cat throwing go back to about 1410, although it may have begun much earlier. The practice took place on what became known as 'cat's Wednesday' in the second week of Lent. The origins of cat throwing are not fully understood, but this type of organised cruelty towards cats was not unusual and similar events took place in many parts of Europe. The cat-throwing tradition in Ypres lasted on and off until 1817, when the last live cat was thrown from the tower. A witness to the event claimed the cat survived the fall and scampered off unharmed.

Caught in a barrel

While the British traditionally scoff pancakes before the fasting season of Lent, the Danes prefer to hit cats trapped in barrels. They eat a lot too, and the festival of Fastelavn celebrates the evening before the fast. Children are entertained with a barrel made of soft balsa wood which is filled with sweets. They can only get their hands on the goodies by hitting the barrel with a stick and the child who successfully makes a hole is crowned king or queen of cats. These days, the only cat involved is the one painted onto the barrel, but until the mid-19th century there was a real cat inside (which, understandably, ran off as soon as an escape hole was made). Beating the barrel was supposed to ward off evil, presumably represented by the unfortunate cat.

Paris cats turned scapegoats

In the 1730s Paris witnessed a sudden outburst of violence against cats which was set off by a group of aggrieved apprentice printers. Conditions for the apprentices were harsh and they apparently felt hard done by compared to the pampered cats belonging to their bosses. Fed up with being kept awake by cats howling near their lodgings, some apprentices decided to take revenge by mewling like cats outside their employer's bedroom. Eventually the printer and his wife could take no more and told the apprentices to destroy the cats, giving strict instructions to save a personal favourite. The apprentices went out and killed every cat they could find in the area around Rue Saint-Séverin, where they worked.

If walls had ears

Another unpleasant belief, which lasted for several hundred years and into the eighteenth century, resulted in the bodies of cats being bricked up inside the walls or placed under the roofs of new buildings. This may have been to ward off evil and keep witches at bay, or simply to drive away mice and rats (the body of a rat is often found alongside the cat). Hundreds of 'dried cats', as they're known, have been found in the walls of old buildings across Britain and other parts of Europe. It's not always easy to say whether these cats were killed first, but the fact that they were often placed in a particular position (something like a pounce action) suggests they were already dead. Much less disturbing are the small wooden figures of cats which have been discovered in houses from the 15th to the 18th centuries, presumably to serve a similarly superstitious purpose.

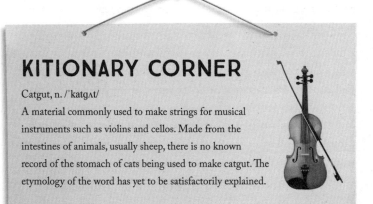

KITIONARY CORNER

Catgut, n. /ˈkatgʌt/
A material commonly used to make strings for musical instruments such as violins and cellos. Made from the intestines of animals, usually sheep, there is no known record of the stomach of cats being used to make catgut. The etymology of the word has yet to be satisfactorily explained.

Eastern promise

Historically, attitudes to cats were generally much more positive in Asian cultures than they were in Europe. Cats were still the stuff of superstition, but they were much more likely to be the bringers of good fortune than bad luck. Thailand is a case in point. The *Tamra Maew* ('cat poems') is an illustrated manuscript which describes 23 different types of cats; 17 of them are lucky, while six are bringers of bad luck. The cat we now know as the Siamese is one of those identified as auspicious. The existing manuscript (in the National Library of Thailand) dates from the early 19th century, but it's believed that versions may have been produced as early as 1350.

The Japanese have also traditionally regarded cats as lucky and there are quite a number of cat shrines in the country, some of them featuring a statue of Nekomata, a mythical feline creature from Japanese folktales. One explanation for this national appreciation of the cat is the important role they played in protecting the silk industry. This valuable cloth was highly vulnerable to gnawing rodents, so pest-control felines were respected for their contribution to the economy.

In Japan, even fishermen regard cats as lucky, despite having good cause to suspect that cats may be after their catch. Traditionally, fishermen on the island of Tashirojima believed they could judge the size of the catch by watching the way cats behaved. Even now, local people believe feeding cats will bring them luck. The island is now sometimes called Cat Island because of its diminishing human population and thriving colony of felines.

Cats are also often in evidence at Buddhist temples throughout Southeast Asia, where they are generally fed, sheltered and treated with kindness. Buddhist belief holds that souls can be born and re-born in both human and animal bodies, which goes some way to explaining why cats in Buddhist cultures have not been subjected to as much persecution as they once were in Christian societies (where tradition has it that only humans have souls). Buddhism teaches that all living creatures should be treated with respect and there has been a long tradition of cats living alongside monks, which continues to this day.

Let sleeping cats lie

Islamic tradition favours cats, which are regarded as pure in spirit and not to be harmed. One legend tells how the Prophet Muhammad cut off the sleeve of his robe rather than disturb his cat, Muezza, who was curled up asleep when he was called to prayer.

In the picture

Although there were times in history when the Church's attitude towards cats was ambivalent or hostile, this wasn't always the case. The Celtic monks of the early Middle Ages kept cats in their monasteries, which were often in remote places. Many of these monks were scribes who produced beautifully decorated illuminated manuscripts, written on vellum. Cats would have been invaluable at protecting this costly material from rodents and, no doubt, would have provided some welcome companionship. We get an inkling of this friendship from a poem written by an Irish monk in the eighth century, which describes how he works alongside 'Pangur Ban my cat'.

Cats also appear frequently on the pages of illuminated manuscripts. One exquisite example is the Lindisfarne Gospels, which was created somewhere around the year 700AD in the island monastery of Lindisfarne. On the initial page of St Luke's Gospel, an elongated cat stretches along the right-hand margin. A chain of birds walk haplessly towards the cat's mouth, and its stomach already contains eight cormorants. Another example is the Book of Kells, which was written around 800. In one image, two mice nibble at the Eucharist under the watchful eyes of a pair of cats. Two more mice have jumped onto the cats' backs. Naturally, the historian will look for the symbolism behind these images – are the cats guardians of good or agents of evil? Whatever their hidden meaning, there is nothing in these images which suggests fear or loathing to the modern viewer. These beautifully drawn cats do not have a particularly malevolent appearance and, although not exactly naturalistic, they do capture a quality of the real-life cats that once made a home in the scriptorium.

A fair price

The monetary value of cats was recognised by the tenth century King Hywel Dda of Wales (or Howell the Good in English) who clarified the value of a cat in his legal codes. 'At birth she is worth a penny,' so goes the law, 'two pence after she has opened her eyes, and a groat if she has caught a mouse.' Hywel also decreed that if a cat was killed, the owner should be compensated with enough grain to cover the dead animal from the tip of the tail to the head. A rare example of recognition for the valuable work done by cats to protect grain supplies.

KITIONARY CORNER

Fatcat, n. /ˈkatɡʌt/

A slang and often derogatory term for a person who has a lot of money which they may use to gain power and favour. Commonly used to describe those who are perceived to be overpaid and out of touch with ordinary people, the term was originally coined in the US in the 1920s and referred to wealthy backers of political parties.

Ten cat lovers in history

Cardinal Thomas Wolsey: Lord Chancellor under Henry VIII before eventually being accused of treason in 1529, Cardinal Wolsey was a cat lover at a time when it could be dangerous to be so. He was said to have had a cat near him most of the time, a fact reflected in a statue in his home town of Ipswich, which features a cat.

Pope Leo XII: One of a number of popes known to have kept cats, Pope Leo had a cat called Micetto that used to sit in the folds of his robe when he gave audiences and was allowed to wander at will around church buildings in the Vatican. When the Pope died in 1829, the cat was left to French writer and diplomat the Vicomte de Chateaubriand.

Jeremy Bentham: The London-born philosopher, eccentric and founder of Utilitarianism is best known for developing the principle of 'the greatest happiness of the greatest number of people'. He was very fond of cats and had a tomcat which he addressed as Reverend John Langbourne. Bentham's preserved skeleton is still in a display case in University College, London, as per instructions written shortly before his death in 1832

Queen Victoria: Queen Victoria was a great animal lover and kept a considerable number of pets throughout her long life. She was particularly fond of dogs, but also took a shine to Persian cats. She owned two, called Flypie and White Heather, which were adopted by her eldest son Edward and his wife Alexandra when the Queen died in 1901.

Florence Nightingale: The nursing pioneer was devoted to cats and kept dozens of them over her lifetime (some of them named after leading politicians of the day, including Bismarck, Disraeli and Gladstone). She is said to have valued their work as rodent catchers during her days nursing soldiers in the Crimea. Some of her cats live on in history, thanks to paw prints on her letters.

Winston Churchill: The wartime leader was drawn to cats and always had at least one at his official residence, as well as others at his private home, Chartwell, in Kent. When the house was given to the National Trust in 1966, his request that there should always be a marmalade tom called Jock living comfortably at the property was honoured. The first Jock was given to Churchill on his 88th birthday. Jock VI took up residence in 2014.

Vladimir Lenin: Vladimir Ilich Ulyanov took the name Lenin in 1901 and went on to become a political theorist and leading figure in the Russian Revolution of 1917. Perhaps an unlikely pet lover, there are in fact quite a number of photographs and even some film footage of the Bolshevik leader petting a cat, apparently with a considerable degree of affection

Edwin Hubble: The American astronomer was the first to observe that the universe was expanding (a fact known as Hubble's law) and has an enormous space telescope named after him. He was also a cat lover and had a cat called Nicolas Copernicus, who spent many hours sprawled out on Hubble's desk or on his lap while he was working.

Nikola Tesla: The inventor and engineer worked with Thomas Edison and made a massive contribution to the alternating-current electrical system. His life's work was inspired by a cat. While stroking his cat, Macak, as a very young child, Tesla became fascinated by what appeared to be sparks coming off the cat's coat. Tesla later said that the experience had inspired a life-long interest in the nature of electricity.

Albert Einstein: The father of modern physics was a believer in kindness towards animals and urged 'widening our circle of compassion' to include all living creatures. He was often surrounded by cats while at work in his study and had one particular cat who apparently became depressed when it rained. 'I know what's wrong, dear fellow,' Einstein was heard to say to the cat, 'but I don't know how to turn it off.'

Across the ocean

Domestic cats were introduced to the Americas by successive waves of settlers who came from Europe and landed in both North and South America. Cats were often taken on the long voyage, both to keep down rodents aboard ship and to hunt rats in the newly settled territories.

Cats in the White House

The First Dog has often been more famous, but there have been a number of cats resident in the White House. One of the first known White House cats was called Tabby and belonged to Abraham Lincoln. Theodore Roosevelt kept a menagerie at the White House, including bears, kangaroos, lizards and snakes. He also had a cat called Tom Quartz and one named Slippers that had six toes. John F. Kennedy had a wide range of pets as well, including Tom Kitten, despite the fact that the president was actually allergic to cats. Bill Clinton's cat, Socks, became one of the best-known First Cats and was frequently photographed by the world's press. Socks was often found in the Oval Office and liked to sit on the President's shoulders. After leaving the White House, Socks enjoyed a long retirement and died in 2009 at the age of twenty.

Cats in the Blitz

When the Second World War broke out, the British government formed the National Air Raid Precautions Animals Committee, which promptly advised the public to send their cats and dogs to the countryside. If that wasn't possible, the advice went, the kindest thing to do was to have your pets destroyed. Owners were warned that pets would not be allowed into air raid shelters and they would not have access to food rations.

Despite the opposition of animal welfare charities like Battersea Dogs & Cats Home (which continued operating throughout the war) hundreds of thousands of animals were put to sleep in the first few days after the declaration of war in 1939. In many cases, people who believed they were doing their patriotic duty took this drastic step with a very heavy heart.

With the bombing of British cities came more danger for pets and many were killed. Others lost their homes (possibly along with their owners) and became strays. Animal welfare organisations did their best to rescue cats and dogs from bombed-out streets, particularly in London during the Blitz, but inevitably many cats were left to fend for themselves, eventually forming feral colonies which became a feature of London life for many years after.

Faith in the city

Stories of animal courage and survival seemed to lift the spirits of many Londoners during the dark days of the Second World War. Stories of brave dogs and plucky felines began appearing in the press during the Blitz, turning at least one cat into a wartime celebrity. Faith was the church cat at the Church of St Augustine's and St Faith's, which stands close to St Paul's Cathedral. One day in September 1940, Faith was seen moving her kitten into a recess in a basement. The vicar repeatedly brought her back to the upstairs vicarage, but she insisted on going back to her shelter. Three days later the church was almost completely destroyed in an air raid. Faith remained in her den and was rescued the next day – mother and kitten were both unharmed. The story about Faith's determination to protect her kitten caught the public imagination and she became an emblem of hope, giving a much needed morale boost to a beleaguered population.

TEN CAT MUSEUMS

There are a number of cat museums around the world to satisfy the cat lover with a thirst for further knowledge about all things felines. Some of them are tiny, one or two of them are a little eccentric, more than one of them claims to be the only cat museum in the world, quite a few have real cats on the premises and all of them are a fabulous testament to a friendship that goes back a long, long way.

De Kattenkabinet (the cat cabinet) in Amsterdam houses a collection of cat-themed art and is also home to a few real-life cats.

The Cat Museum in San Francisco organises 'pop-up' exhibitions around the city on themes such as cats in Japanese art and felines on film.

The Feline Historical Museum in Alliance, Ohio, has an extensive collection of lucky Japanese cats and you're quite likely to bump into a Maine Coon or a Ragdoll strolling about the place.

The Kuching Cat Museum in Malaysia has over 4000 feline artefacts, including some that were previously held at the National Museum in Kuala Lumpur.

Singapore's Lion City Kitty cat museum features catty art and crafts from around the world and doubles up as a rescue shelter and re-homing centre.

Moscow Cat Museum has a wide range of cat-inspired art and objects and has exhibitions on cats in Russia, as well as one on the special relationship between women and cats.

St Petersburg has its own Cat Museum, which has exhibitions on cats in the city's history and celebrates the feline muses to artists, writers and musicians. The museum even has a cat-friendly cafe nearby.

The Cats Museum in Kotor, Montenegro, has an impressive collection of prints, postcards, advertisements and labels featuring cats and even some very old invoices with cat designs.

The Cat Museum in Siauliai, Lithuania, has a large collection of cat-themed items from all over the world. There are figures in porcelain, amber, crystal and marble and even stained-glass windows and lamps.

The Maneki Neko Museum in Seto, Japan (a town famous for its ceramics), has several thousand pottery cats on display, as well as information about the history of Japan's lucky beckoning cat.

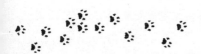

CAT AND MOUSE

Felines at work

Cats are not widely regarded as the most useful of animals. They have a reputation for being a bit lazy and not particularly eager to please. Granted, they can't be trained to assist the disabled or find a cache of illegal drugs, but the one thing they can do, they do very well – catching rodents. True, cats are not very flexible when it comes to their line of work, but they'll do their job virtually anywhere. Cats have worked on farms, on ships, in factories and mills, in public buildings and private homes. The modern cat owner probably finds this talent for mousing a bit of a nuisance, but for much of history, mice and rats posed a serious threat to food and other goods, as well as human health, so perhaps we should show greater appreciation for the valuable role cats have played when it comes to vermin control.

Feline retrievers?

The ancient Egyptians certainly appreciated cats for their hunting skills, but could they have trained cats to retrieve game? A number of tomb paintings put a cat at the heart of a hunting party. Typically, the scene depicts the deceased alongside family members on a waterfowl hunt, in which a cat appears to be taking part. One particularly striking example is from the tomb of Nebamun, which was painted about 1450 BC and is now in the British Museum. Nebamun is standing on a small boat in marshland, his wife and child next to him. A cat by his side seems to be dispatching three birds at once.

These images have led some to wonder if the Egyptians actually trained their cats to retrieve game. Others have speculated that the cats may have been taken on the hunt in order to flush the birds out, or perhaps cause a distraction. But Egyptian art was often highly symbolic, so it could be a mistake to interpret these images too literally. When scenes like those found on Nebamun's tomb were painted, cats were an integral part of domestic life, so Nebamun is shown accompanied by his whole family: wife, child and cat. This doesn't necessarily mean that any of them would have taken part in a real-life hunting trip and it certainly doesn't prove that cats were trained to retrieve. What it does do, however, is highlight once again just how central cats were to Egyptian life.

All aboard

The life of a sailor was often a harsh one. Months on end with nothing but ocean to look at, not much fresh food and no word from loved ones at home. On top of all that were the many irritations caused by tiny stowaways: mice in your bed, rats gnawing at the rigging and lines of little droppings in your stale breakfast bread. No wonder cats were often press-ganged into service by seafarers. Cats are not naturally drawn to water, but they've been at sea since ancient times, transported around the world by explorers, traders and conquerors.

Because of their useful work, cats on ships were generally regarded as lucky and their behaviour was closely observed for signs of changes in weather conditions. The contribution cats made to maritime endeavours was largely unsung for many millennia, but the 20th century saw a number of cats turned into minor celebrities for their work during the Second World War and in the course of various Polar explorations. In conflict situations, the role of the cat was more than just rodent control. Cats became mascots, and their presence could create a sense of normality and be a great source of comfort to navy recruits, who were often very young and away from home for the first time in extremely stressful circumstances.

Oskar of the Bismarck

The adventures of one particular cat in the Second World War became the stuff of legend. Oskar was the ship's cat on the *Bismarck* when the German battleship was sunk in 1941. He apparently survived and was picked up by crew members on HMS *Cossack*, which was also hit a few months later. Oskar (who was renamed *Unsinkable Sam* at some point during all of these exploits) then found himself on the aircraft carrier HMS *Ark Royal*. After a few more near misses at sea, he ended up with a desk-bound job with the Governor of Gibraltar. Later returned to the United Kingdom, it's said that *Unsinkable Sam* lived out his retirement in a seaman's home in Northern Ireland. If all of this seems a bit far-fetched, it's because this heroic tale of survival is almost certainly exaggerated, embellished or patched together from other stories, with varying degrees of attachment to the truth. It's not that anyone deliberately made up the story; it just grew naturally out of a series of real events. There is a portrait of Oskar/Unsinkable Sam in the National Maritime Museum in Greenwich, London, which isn't bad going for a cat who may not even have existed. Perhaps it's best to set aside the dubious veracity of *Unsinkable Sam's* life story and instead see the painting as a tribute to all the very real cats that went to sea during the Second World War.

On the Discovery

When Captain Scott set off for the Antarctic in 1901 on his first expedition to the South Pole he had a crew of 38 men with him on his ship, the *Discovery,* as well as 25 sled dogs and a Scottish terrier called Scamp. The ship also had two cats, called Blackwell and Poplar. The ship became trapped in ice through two winters in 1902 and 1903, before being rescued by the crews of two other ships, who used dynamite to free the ship from the ice. Towards the end of the ordeal, Poplar was tragically killed by the half-starved sled dogs. Blackwell, however, had a happier fate and was still in one piece when the *Discovery* reached New Zealand in April 1904.

KITIONARY CORNER

Mouser, n. /ˈmaʊsə/

In Old English a musere was a bird of prey that dined on mice. Variants of the word have been used to describe cats as well as birds since the 1400s. The word is still commonly used to describe cats with a predilection for hunting.

Book worms

Books have always been made of stuff that rodents love to gnaw, be it paper, papyrus, parchment or vellum. This makes libraries particularly vulnerable to mice and rat infestations. Not surprisingly then, there"s a long tradition of encouraging cats to hang around libraries, temples, monasteries, court archives and anywhere else where important texts, documents and manuscripts are stored. It's a tradition which started in the ancient world and still goes on to this day, although modern library cats are perhaps more appreciated for raising a smile than their ability to catch mice between the shelves.

One famous example is Dewey Readmore Books, who was the resident library cat in the small town of Spencer in Iowa, USA, until his death in 2006 at the age of nineteen. Dewey (named after the Dewey Decimal Classification System used by librarians) became something of a celebrity in his lifetime and has since been the subject of a best-selling biography. Rodents may not trouble our libraries quite as much as they once did, but there are still a few cats hanging around libraries across the world today, to help you choose a good book to curl up with.

Guardians of the Hermitage

The State Hermitage in St Petersburg, Russia, has been home to cats since the Empress Elizabeth Petrovna (daughter of Peter the Great) put out a decree in 1745 calling for the best ratters in Russia to be brought to the palace. There were cats at the Hermitage throughout the Napoleonic wars and the Russian Revolution, but they didn't survive the terrible siege of what was then Leningrad during the Second World War. Cats were re-instated when peace was restored, and they've lived there ever since. Now one of the biggest and best-known museums in the world, the Hermitage is home to around seventy cats, all looked after by volunteers and funded by public donations. There is even a cat hospital on site. They are not allowed in the exhibition areas, but they roam freely in other parts of the extensive buildings. Cats at the Hermitage are no longer expected to catch rats, but they do often pose for tourist photos.

Special delivery

You might expect the Royal Mail to be diligent about paperwork and to do things by the letter, and you'd be right. Indeed, it is this very punctilious approach to their records which has delivered us some very detailed accounts of feline employees at the Post Office. Unlike many other places of work, cats didn't just do the odd bit of casual work at post offices – they were actually officially on the payroll for over a hundred years. Payments were carefully recorded and much of the correspondence regarding Post Office cats still exists in archives today.

Cloth mail sacks were easy for rodents to get their teeth into and it wasn't unusual for letters and valuable postal orders to end up in shreds. People also sent food parcels through the post, an obvious temptation. Using poison around private mail was clearly a risk, so cats seemed like the perfect solution. The first three cats to be appointed by the Post Office began work at the Money Order Office in London in 1868, in the wake of a particularly bad mouse infestation. They were given an allowance of one shilling a week. The initiative was obviously a success and soon allowances were been given to other post offices for the maintenance of a growing staff of cats. The tradition came to an end when Blackie, the last cat to work at Post Office Headquarters, died in 1984.

Corridors of power

Many places of work have long since abandoned the once widespread practice of keeping a mouser on the premises, opting instead for chemical, mechanical or sonic solutions to rodent problems. But there is one place where the tradition still holds: Downing Street. The current holder of the title Chief Mouser to the Cabinet Office is Larry, a former Battersea Dogs & Cats Home resident, who has held the post since 2011. Initially, Larry received criticism from the press for being a bit slack on the job and was frequently photographed doing not much at all, but he has since proved himself by dutifully dispatching a few mice for the cameras.

Treading the boards

Theatres, with their old, crumbling buildings and backstage warrens, are ideal locations for rodents. Bring on the feline thespians who have patrolled the wings and dressing rooms of theatres for many years. There once was a time when virtually every theatre in Britain would have had a resident cat, a tradition celebrated by T. S. Eliot with his character Gus the Theatre Cat, who appears in *Old Possum's Book of Practical Cats*. There were still theatre cats well into the 1970s and 80s, but as the last generation reached retirement, the practice was slowly phased out. There were practical concerns about having animals running about the place, as well as questions about whether this theatrical lifestyle was really in the best interests of the cats. The consensus was that cats should live in a family home and not be left to their own devices in a cavernous building, with no one in particular taking primary responsibility for them. The rodents, however, have not left the building. Mice and rats, it seems, are still having a wild old time in theatreland. The actor's union, Equity, even launched a campaign to re-introduce cats to London's ageing theatres in a bid to reduce the damage caused by rodents and boost morale among performers.

Moscow circus cats

Generally, theatre cats operate behind the scenes, but occasionally they take centre stage. Moscow residents and visitors to the city can enjoy the unusual (and perhaps a little uncomfortable) spectacle of performing cats. Around 120 cats and a handful of humans make up the cast at Moscow Cats Theatre, where cats walk tightropes, spin balls, jump on shoulders and generally clown around.

TEN FAMOUS PROFESSIONAL FELINES

Blackie the ship's cat: Assigned to HMS *Prince of Wales* during the Second World War, Blackie was aboard when Winston Churchill sailed to Newfoundland for a secret meeting with Franklin D. Roosevelt. As Churchill was about to disembark, Blackie sauntered by, earning a gentle stroke from the cat-loving prime minister. Promptly renamed Churchill, Blackie survived the sinking of the *Prince of Wales* later that year and was taken to Singapore. When Singapore was evacuated in 1942, Blackie could not be found and his fate is unknown.

Mike the museum cat: Between 1909 and 1929 Mike was on duty at the main gate of the British Museum. He was brought to the museum by resident cat Black Jack, who deposited a tiny kitten at the feet of the curator of Egyptian antiquities, Sir Ernest A. T. Wallis Budge. Mike was fond of catching pigeons and was particularly adept at terrifying passing dogs. When Mike died, he was given an obituary in the *London Evening Standard* and Sir Wallis Budge wrote a pamphlet about him, detailing key events in the cat's life.

Felix the ship's cat: In 1620, the *Mayflower* set sail from Plymouth for America in what was to become a defining event in America's history. In 1957, a replica ship – called *Mayflower II* – repeated the journey. A small kitten called Felix joined the crew. A tiny lifejacket was made for him, which he didn't take to, but he soon found his sea legs, despite being startled by flying fish landing on board. Feted by the media on arrival in America, Felix settled in Massachusetts.

Tibs the Post Office cat: Stationed in the refreshment club at Post Office Headquarters, Tibs worked for the Post Office for fourteen years until his death in 1964. Nicknamed Tibs the Great, he grew rather large (thanks, presumably, to helpings from the dining room and not just mice) and weighed 23lb. When he died, an obituary was published in the *Post Office Magazine*.

Tiddles the station cat: Tiddles had an unusual job for a cat. For many years he was feline attendant in the ladies' loo at Paddington Station. He was adopted as a six-week-old stray by a woman who worked as an attendant and quickly became a fixture. He gained a growing band of admirers, who would donate food for his upkeep. His unhealthy lifestyle led to weight gain and by 1982 he weighed 32lb. He died in 1983 at the age of thirteen.

Beerbohm the theatre cat: Resident mouser at London's Globe Theatre (now the Gielgud), Beerbohm (named after the famous actor-manager, Herbert Beerbohm) wandered at will into dressing rooms and occasionally even across the stage during a performance. He died in 1995, aged almost twenty, and remains the only cat to have been honoured with an obituary in the actor's newspaper *The Stage*.

Humphrey the Downing Street cat: Humphrey was found as a stray by a civil servant in 1989. He went on to serve as Downing Street mouser under three prime ministers. Never far from the headlines, Humphrey was falsely accused of killing a family of robins in 1994. A year later he went missing, only to turn up at the Royal Army Medical College, where they assumed he was a stray. Humphrey retired in 1997 on grounds of ill health.

Rusik the sniffer cat: Rusik was recruited by Russian police to detect hidden stashes of illegally caught sturgeon. These valuable fish (which produce caviar) live in the Caspian Sea, where poaching is a serious and constant threat. Rusik was adopted by police as a kitten and was trained to sniff out fish in spot checks on vehicles. Tragically, Rusik was killed by a car in his first year of service in 2003. Police suspect Rusik may have been deliberately targeted by smugglers.

Tama the station cat: Tama was credited with saving a rural train line from financial ruin when she became honorary stationmaster at Kishi station in western Japan after the last human employee was laid off to save money. Decked out in a stationmaster's hat, Tama became an unexpected draw and passenger numbers shot up. Tama greeted visitors as they got off trains and became a Japanese celebrity. When she died in 2015, 3000 mourners attended her Shinto-style funeral.

Felix the station cat: Felix joined the team at Huddersfield station in Yorkshire when she was a kitten in 2011. After patrolling the platforms for mice for five years, and winning the hearts of passengers, she was promoted in 2016 to Senior Pest Controller. A cat flap has been built into one of ticket barriers so she can go about her duties and she has been issued with a high-visibility jacket and name badge befitting her professional status.

Cats in space

As far as we know, there are no mice in space, but that didn't stop scientists from sending a couple of cats on a suborbital flight. Uncertain as to what the effects of space travel on humans might be, a number of different animal species have been sent rocketing in the name of space exploration. Monkeys, dogs, fruit flies, mealworms and bullfrogs have all made the journey (although not all of them made it back). The only cats to be astronauts were trained by French rocket scientists in the 1960s. The cats selected were apparently strays and training involved living in confined spaces and being strapped into centrifuges and compression chambers. In October 1963, a cat called Félicette was taken to a rocket base in Algeria, strapped into her spacecraft and launched into the air. The flight lasted about 15 minutes and reached an altitude of 130 miles. Félicette parachuted back down to earth, miraculously unharmed.

AT YOUR SERVICE

Making life easier for cats

Cats don't have much use for material goods. They might appreciate a few toys or a soft bed to sleep on (although yours will do just as well) and they may tolerate wearing a collar, but generally they're not big on accessorising. All most cats really need is some tasty food and a bit of peace. Their owners, by contrast, love shopping, and money makes our world go round, so we're forever developing new products and buying extra kit for our cats. We love innovation and generally try to make things better than they used to be. Our ideas develop and change too, which is why the way we treat cats has changed so much. This inventiveness has often made life better and easier for our cats and can give them longer, happier, healthier lives.

Making an entrance

There's one home improvement in particular that makes living together much more pleasant for human and cat alike: the cat flap. There's an often repeated story that Sir Isaac Newton, the great physicist and mathematician, actually invented the cat flap. The story goes that when his experimental work was repeatedly interrupted by a cat scratching at the door to be let in, Newton hit upon the idea of cutting a hole in the door so the cat could come and go freely. Now, the evidence for this theory is a lot more shaky than Newton's actual great discovery, gravity (or the theory that if you drop things, they fall to the ground).

In the first place, sawing a hole in a door is not quite the same thing as inventing the cat flap (the genius of the cat flap being, of course, that it closes, stopping great gusts of wind blowing through your home). Secondly, there was nothing particularly unusual about holes for cats in buildings. Barns, outbuildings and farmhouses often had them to allow cats to go about their important work as pest controllers (they were particularly common in rural Spain, where they are called *gateras*).

Of course, it's perfectly possible that Newton did create a little entrance for his cat, but not everything a scientist does is an invention. Nobody's quite sure where this story about Newton and the cat flap came from or why it has endured. At least one of Newton's Three Laws of Motion must be in play when it comes to the workings of the modern cat flap, closing,

as they do, by themselves after a cat has walked through. Nowadays, they can even be operated by a magnet on the cat's collar or a microchip buried under the cat's skin. This latest innovation solves the two-fold drawback of the original hole-in-the-door concept, keeping out draughts as well as every stray Tom, Dick and Harry in the neighbourhood.

KITIONARY CORNER

Cattery, n. /ˈkatəri/

Used to describe a place where cats are housed or bred since 1790. Now most commonly used to describe an establishment where cats can be left while their owners are away.

TEN GREAT IDEAS THAT HAVE MADE LIFE BETTER FOR CATS

ANIMAL PROTECTION LAWS: The Protection of Animals Act was introduced in 1911 and outlawed unnecessary suffering and deliberate acts of cruelty.

VACCINATIONS: Prevention is better than cure and many fatal conditions have been prevented since the development of routine vaccinations for cats.

NEUTERING: The advent of safe, humane operations to prevent unwanted litters of kittens has done more than almost anything else to improve cat welfare.

QUICK-RELEASE CAT COLLARS: A simple device that allows cats to carry ID without the risk of becoming trapped in a potentially fatal situation.

CATNIP TOYS: The cat's (safe) drug of choice wrapped up in mouse form. A feline pleasure dome in a small and very affordable package.

RADIATOR BEDS: Cats love being cosy and warm (and high up), so making a bed that fits on a radiator is an ingenious design innovation.

SCRATCHING POSTS: Cats need to scratch, but people prefer sofas without shreds. Strategically placed scratching posts can keep everyone happy.

MAGNETIC CAT FLAPS: The ideal solution to giving your pet the freedom to come and go without letting in neighbourhood cat burglars.

CAT SITTERS: Be they friend or professional, a reliable person to feed your cat while you're away means your cat can spend the holiday where they're happiest – at home.

DUTY OF CARE: The Animal Welfare Act of 2006 makes all animal owners responsible for making sure the welfare needs of their animals are met.

Doing your business

It's not always the most exciting things that make the biggest difference. Cat litter, for instance, is not going to light anyone's fire. Yet, if you think about it, the litter tray is an essential item for the modern domestic cat. Even if your cat goes outside a lot of the time, there are always moments in a cat's life when they need to be kept in (illness, fireworks, old age and so on). Without decent cat litter, this would be a bit of a faff – and not a very pleasant one at that.

But cat litter doesn't just exist. Someone had to give it a name, get it packaged and persuade shops to stock it. That person was Ed Lowe, who worked in his father's delivery business in Michigan, USA. His first (not so great) idea was to sell fuller's earth (a type of clay) to chicken farmers. When that didn't really get off the ground, he found himself with rather a lot of the stuff. With the help of a neighbour's cat, he discovered that fuller's earth could absorb not just liquid but even the smell of cat pee. Before that, people had used sand or earth if they needed to provide an indoor toilet for a cat.

In 1947, Lowe began selling what he called 'Kitty Litter'. In 1954, he launched 'Tidy Cat', this time aimed at the mass market and hitting the shelves just as supermarkets were taking off. To cut a long story short, in 1990 Lowe sold his company for $200 million, making him one of those self-made businessmen who made a fortune by selling us something we didn't even know we needed. It's even been suggested that the success of Lowe's product had a significant impact on pet-keeping habits in America. Absorbent cat litter made keeping a cat (particularly an indoor pet) more appealing and helped to turn the cat from a little-regarded outside animal to a proper member of the family.

These days, there is a dizzying array of cat litters on offer, made from a wide range of materials. You can choose from clay, wood pellets, recycled paper, silica gel, walnut shells or whole-kernel corn, and people will have an opinion on clumping and non-clumping varieties. Cleaning the litter tray may be less smelly these days, but shopping has not got any easier.

On the menu

For much of the time humans and cats have been living together, cats were expected to get their own food; indeed, that was the main reason we wanted them around in the first place. People have often put out scraps to encourage cats to settle near mice-infested buildings, but it was feared that feeding them too much would put them off their work.

As cats crept from the barn into the home, we took on more responsibility for them. A plate of scraps and a saucer of milk would have

been a normal addition to a cat's diet of mice and rats. In the 19th century, pet food could be bought from the cats' meat man, a familiar sight in the streets of London and other large cities. These small-scale traders would push a barrow round selling meat for cats and dogs, which was generally unfit for human (or even animal) consumption, usually horsemeat. This practice seems to have continued throughout the 19th century and on into the 1920s or 1930s, overlapping with the very beginnings of commercial pet food production.

The first mass-produced pet food product was Spratt's dog biscuits, named after the American entrepreneur James Spratt, who launched his biscuits in London around 1860. Sold with the help of some shrewd marketing techniques and some very appealing billboards, Spratt's became the leading commercial pet food brand for many years, selling food and other products for dogs, cats, birds and fish. Since then, of course, it's become a very crowded market and the modern cat owner is spoilt for choice when they come to the pet food aisle in the supermarket. Sadly, this has led in part to a very modern problem – feline obesity. It's thought that over a quarter of our cats are dangerously overweight, which has led in turn to yet another product for cats: diet food.

The doctor will see you now

The vet is not usually a cat's favourite person, but they should probably be a bit more appreciative. Veterinary medicine has come on in leaps and bounds in recent years and the treatments routinely available now would have been unthinkable only a short time ago. There were specialists in

 animal medicine way back in 3000 BC, when the treatment of animals was described in Mesopotamia. The modern veterinary profession, though, began in 1761, when a school was founded in Lyon, France. The London Veterinary College was founded in 1791, when the most pressing issue was the health of military horses.

When William Dick established a veterinary school in Edinburgh in 1823, this pioneering establishment was primarily concerned with horses, cattle, sheep and pigs. Dogs got a bit of a look in too, but cats were not generally considered important enough to worry about. In the early days, veterinarians struggled to get their craft recognised as a valuable science, so they concentrated on animals that were economically useful. Vets were not for pets, but for farmers.

This fact is clearly reflected in the writings of James Alfred Wight, who wrote under the pen name James Herriot and became a household name thanks to the popular TV series *All Creatures Great and Small*. The first of his stories begins in 1937, when the newly qualified Herriot joins a practice in the Yorkshire Dales. Herriot's boss, Siegfried Farnon, is a moderniser and keen to expand his small-animal clientele, although he's fighting ingrained attitudes in the profession which see cats and dogs as unworthy patients.

The James Herriot books (and subsequent TV series) perfectly capture a moment of change for the veterinarian profession. Agriculture had once been a vet's bread and butter, but pet owners were increasingly prepared to pay for their animal's health. The vets in *All Creatures Great and Small* have their hands up a cow one minute and are grappling with Boris the cat the next.

CATS IN MYTH AND LEGEND

Felines of fantasy and imagination

Ever since they first snuck into an outbuilding or took up residence in a barn, cats have been quietly minding their own business and getting on with the things that cats do, mainly dozing, stalking, napping, making kittens, hunting, washing themselves and a bit more sleeping. Humans, by contrast, have been busily projecting all sorts of fancies and fantasies onto these perfectly normal creatures. Faced with a cat, the human imagination seems to go into overdrive. The cat's nocturnal antics (often accompanied by piercing shrieks) and their responsiveness to sounds we humans cannot hear may have contributed to this air of mystery. Amazed by these seemingly otherworldly creatures, we have created no end of myths, legends and superstitions about a species that still inspires both awe and anxiety.

Turn again, Whittington

Dick Whittington's cat plays a pivotal role in the well-known rags to riches tale of a poor orphan boy who went to London to make his fortune and ended up becoming Lord Mayor. Somewhere along the way, Dick Whittington's cat (with or without his owner, depending on which version you're reading) travels to the Barbary Coast (or thereabouts) and makes a fortune by impressing the king (or the sultan), whose palace had been plagued by rats before this expert mouser arrived.

This folktale has been told and re-told since it first appeared around the 17th century. It's been presented as a drama, turned into a ballad, written in prose as a fairy tale and performed as a puppet show and even an opera. Modern audiences will be most familiar with the pantomime version, still a firm favourite in the festive season. Like many folktales, there is a kernel of truth at the heart of this legend, but, sadly, the cat's contribution to the story is pure fabrication. The poor boy turned rich part is also untrue. Richard Whittington was, indeed, Lord Mayor of London. In fact, he was Lord Mayor of London four times, between 1397 and 1419. He was not, however, from an impoverished background. From a wealthy family, he became a successful businessman in his own right, making his fortune as a cloth merchant and money lender. He was also a philanthropist who donated large sums to civic projects in the city, but there is no evidence that he had a cat.

Quite why and how the cat snuck into the story, no one quite knows, although it may be telling that similar folktales about cats helping poor boys to become rich exist in other parts of Europe. Another interesting facet of the Dick Whittington legend is that this tale with a cat at its heart emerged at a time when cats were still associated with witchcraft, which just goes to show that our attitudes to cats have never been simply black and white.

Paws up

The Maneki Neko, or Lucky Beckoning Cat, originated in Japan and went on to be much appreciated in China too. In fact, there's almost certain to be one in a takeaway near you, probably in ceramic or plastic form. Maneki Neko is usually a white cat wearing a red collar, with big, appealing eyes and one raised paw. Although most commonly white with red and black patches (basically, a calico cat), these lucky cats do appear in other colours – all symbolising different qualities. Red or pink, for instance, is for luck in love and gold (naturally) brings wealth and prosperity. The Lucky Beckoning Cat can be found on all sorts of trinkets, from stickers and key rings to money boxes and tattoo stencils. In Japan and China they are believed to bring good fortune to businesses by drawing in customers, which is why they are so often placed in the windows of shops and restaurants.

The story of the Maneki Neko began long before the mass-produced knick-knack. The talismanic feline figures emerged in Japan around 1800, near the end of the Edo period. Originally, they were made out of wood, stone or porcelain and later appeared in prints and drawings. The Japanese had long respected cats for their work in protecting the lucrative silk industry from rodents and also had a tendency to credit cats with mystical powers.

There are many versions of the Maneki Neko legend, but the basic plot goes something like this: a cat is given shelter in a humble temple, shop or restaurant by an impoverished individual. This kindness is rewarded with a reversal of fortunes. The Gotoku-ji temple in Tokyo is dedicated to cats and is the source of one of the earliest versions of the tale. According to the legend, the dilapidated temple was saved from ruin by a monk's cat that beckoned a Samurai away from a tree moments before it was struck by lightning. The grateful Samurai made sure that the temple was well rewarded.

Strike it lucky

Everybody knows that walking under ladders is unlucky. Similarly, whether you believe in such folk wisdom or not, you will know about the dangers of broken mirrors and the benefits of touching wood. But what about black cats? Are they good or bad? Should you stay out of their path or hope they walk right in front of you? We seem to have got in a bit of a muddle on this question. The black cat often features on good-luck cards (possibly sitting on a four-leaf clover), but there it is again at Halloween, consorting with things that go bump in the night.

So are black cats lucky or not? Turning to primary sources doesn't do much to clear up the matter. Dictionaries of superstitions, which draw on published texts as well as recorded oral tradition, reveal that there has been centuries of confusion as to whether cats called Jet or Ebony or Sooty should be considered friend or foe. In 1797, an encounter with some black cats on the way to market was enough to make one person go straight back home, but a report from 1907 describes how football teams took a black cat with them onto the pitch for luck. An 1866 source tells us that sailors' wives in Scarborough kept black cats to protect their husbands at sea, but only a few years later, in 1890, oral history tells us that women, in particular, dreaded meeting a black cat.

There's no consensus about whether you would want to meet a black cat early in the morning or on your wedding day (events which have been reported as both very desirable and highly inauspicious). A black cat moving into your house may bring prosperity, but luck could go either way if the same cat crosses your path. Even as late 1957, the issue was still causing considerable confusion. One dictionary of superstitions cites a 12-year-old boy who is recorded as saying, ' The front of a black cat is lucky, the back unlucky.'

In the US and many parts of Europe, black cats are unlucky due to a faintly lingering association with the devil and dark goings on. In Britain, black cats are lucky for more or less exactly the same reason. The thinking goes that if you survive an encounter with one of these devilish creatures without mishap, you must be lucky because nothing bad happened to you. Good luck or bad, these widespread superstitions underline just how much power we have projected onto cats, particularly black ones.

TEN CAT SUPERSTITIONS

Cats have been the subject of more superstitions than probably any other animal. These snippets of folk wisdom are often contradictory and reveal highly conflicting attitudes towards an animal which is at once familiar and strange, both ordinary and uncanny. Few people put much store by such baseless beliefs any more, but they are part of our (and the cat's) heritage. Here are ten superstitions that are best taken with a pinch of salt.

It is very unfortunate to meet a black cat early in the morning.

It is a good omen if a cat runs before a fisherman on his way to the fishing.

Whenever the cat of the house is black, the lasses of lovers will have no lack.

Nine hairs from a black cat, soaked in water, will cure whooping cough.

It is lucky to see a black cat on your way to church to be married.

It is unlucky to meet a cat on your wedding morning.

If a cat sneezes, you will have good luck.

If a cat sneezes three times, you will suffer illness.

If a cat dies inside the house, it will bring bad luck.

It is unlucky to have a cat in the house when someone has died.

Sunny spells and sudden showers

Cats are not that fond of getting wet, but that doesn't make them expert meteorologists. Still, one of the most widespread superstitions about cats involves closely observing their behaviour for signs of imminent changes in the weather. Some beliefs have it that cats can actually change the weather, others regard cats simply as a reliable barometer. Cats are sensitive to changes in heat, light and atmospheric pressure, so there may be something behind these superstitions, but humans have tended to stretch an observable fact to breaking point and placed rather more trust in the cat's forecasting powers than is strictly scientific.

Weather conditions are obviously crucially important to people who go to sea, so sailors and fishermen have been more prone than most to put faith in the skills of feline weathervanes. A cat overboard was believed to whip up a wind and an agitated or frisky cat on a ship was seen as a sign of an approaching storm. Back on land, in coastal communities, a cat going wild and tearing at things was also a sign that the weather at sea was about to turn bad. Cats sneezing, scratching furniture, turning their tail to a fire, washing their face with a paw, cleaning their ears, licking their tail, looking

KITIONARY CORNER

Caterwaul, v. /ˈkatəwɔːl/

Chaucer used a variant of this word to describe the noise cats make while mating, and it may come from a German dialect term, meaning to cry like a cat. It is still used to refer to the noise cats make, but is also more generally applied to loud, discordant sounds produced by people, particularly poor singers.

out of the window, dashing about the place and clawing at things have all been seen as signs that bad weather is to come. In short, unless your cat is asleep, whatever they are doing means you need to take an umbrella with you.

Coming for dinner

The number thirteen is in strong contention with the black cat for the title of most widely feared by the superstitious. Some passengers won't sit in row thirteen on a plane and some hotels number their rooms from twelve to fourteen, skipping number thirteen altogether. Convention has it that thirteen guests at dinner is particularly unfortunate (possibly because Judas Iscariot was supposedly the thirteenth guest at the Last Supper) and should be avoided at any costs. With perhaps a hint of irony, the Savoy Hotel in London came up with the perfect solution by playing two superstitions off against each other. Since 1926, a carved figure of a black cat, known as Kaspar, has taken the place of the fourteenth guest should an inauspicious party of thirteen find themselves dining together.

This particular hotel first went the extra mile to avoid thirteen diners in 1898, after one diner (who would have been the fourteenth person at the table if it hadn't been for a last-minute cancellation) was subsequently shot dead.

Initially, a member of staff joined the table, but diners felt this compromised their privacy. Absolutely silent and utterly discreet, Kaspar the cat proved to be the perfect solution. Kaspar has a full place-setting laid out for him and wears a napkin during the course of the meal. Kaspar is still in service to this day and the Savoy's dining room – once called the River Restaurant – is now called Kaspar's.

Nine lives

Many a cat has taken a giant leap but landed steadily, or come through
a seemingly death-defying scrape still looking cool and unruffled. This
extraordinary acrobatic ability probably goes part way to explaining the cat's
proverbial nine lives, or at least why the idea still resonates. We're bound to
be impressed by (and envious of) how easily cats manage manoeuvres that
would leave us clumsy bipeds in a bit of a mess. But why nine, and where
does such an odd idea come from?

As with many proverbs, we just don't know. Nine, as it happens, is a very
special number which is often invoked in both religion and folklore. It's a
trinity of trinities (three times three) and people once put much more store
in the symbolism of numbers than we do nowadays. The first recorded use of
the concept that a cat has nine lives only goes back to the mid-16th century,
but there are theories that the idea is linked to ancient Egypt. The sun god
Atum-Ra (who sometimes took the form of a cat) embodied the lives of
the nine gods, represented collectively as the Ennead. We all know the
Egyptians made much of cats, but it may be a bit of a stretch to trace this
particular proverb all the way back to such a distant past.

Fairy-cat of the Highlands

The Cait Sith of Celtic legend is a fairy-cat that haunts the Highlands of
Scotland. Possibly inspired by the real-life Scottish wildcat (an elusive and
mysterious creature), the Cait Sith is usually black with a white patch on its
chest. Leaving milk out for the magical feline is a good idea (you could be
cursed if you don't), but it may still steal your soul. In some versions of the
myth, Cait Sith is a witch who can turn herself into a cat eight times. If she
becomes a cat for a ninth time, she will stay that way forever.

Time for a change

A cat one minute, a beautiful woman the next, or perhaps a witch or a demon. This is the kind of thing cats get up to in the often vivid imagination of humans. It's not just cats that can change form; shape-shifting myths about various animals transforming themselves into people (or the other way round) are common to many cultures and have endured from the earliest times to the modern day. Cats have been changing shape (usually into female form) from the time of the Greek fabulist Aesop, to the 1940s, when the horror film *Cat People* was released (the improbable premise of this Hollywood film is that a woman will turn into a cat if she is kissed).

Along the way, there were the ever-changing cats of the witch scares of Europe, and demon cats turning themselves into women in Japanese folklore. One example is the story of the witch-cat of Okabe, which was re-enacted in kabuki theatrical performances in the 19th century. The tale describes how the witch-cat turns herself into a kindly old lady and goes about scaring people. In another Japanese folktale, a cat demon appears as a beautiful seductress and brings about the demise of a feudal lord. Shape-shifting cats are not confined to history either. Were-cats (a term which seems to have first appeared in the 1970s) pop up from time to time in cartoons, teen films and comics.

Venus and the cat

One example of the cat shape-shifter in folktales comes in one of Aesop's fables. 'Venus and the Cat' tells the story of a cat who falls in love with a young man. Knowing he will not return her affections, the cat asks Venus to transform her into a beautiful woman. The man, of course, falls madly in love with her and they marry. Venus, however, has a trick up her sleeve. To see if the cat has really changed, she releases a mouse into the bed chamber.

KITIONARY CORNER

Catty, adj. /ˈkati/

Sometimes used to talk about qualities pertaining
to cats, but commonly used since the 1880s to
describe being deliberately (but often subtly)
unkind or insulting. This slang term is usually,
but not exclusively, used about women.

The husband is not too impressed at the sight of his wife pouncing on the
mouse and Venus turns her back into a cat.

Truth will out

Superstition has it that an injury suffered by the animal version of a shape-
shifting being will still be evident when the creature reverts to human
form. One thread which runs through a number of folktales from different
parts of the world is how a wounded cat leads to inescapable evidence of a
woman's sneaky shape-shifting. A typical example has a woodman working
in the wilds away from home. When his breakfast is repeatedly stolen by a
cat, he catches the animal and cuts off a paw. When he returns home he is
horrified to discover that his wife is now missing a hand. Variations on this
theme reveal unfaithful fiancées, deceitful wives and, of course, witches.

Northern flights

According to Norse mythology, Freya was the goddess of love, beauty
and fertility, and she flew around the sky on a chariot pulled by two cats.

Freya was associated with both love and war and could be gentle as well as ferocious, much like cats. These qualities were valued in the Viking tradition of Scandinavia, but Freya's connection with magical cats was bad news for real cats when Christian culture arrived and tried to banish the beliefs and practices that had gone before. Goddesses of love (and their cats) were pushed to one side and became something to fear and avoid. The cult of Freya, which had respected cats, was replaced by a rejection of Freya's magic and a suspicion of the animals she was so closely associated with.

On the wild side

Around 2000 big cat sightings are reported every year in the UK, which either means there are a lot more panthers, lions and pumas out there than we might have expected (the only native big cat, the lynx, is believed to have become extinct about 1300 years ago), or that some people are letting their imaginations run away with them. The trouble is, glimpsed from afar, it can be difficult to distinguish a big cat from an ordinary-sized domestic one. If viewed in an open field, there may be nothing to give perspective to a cat-shaped creature, so it's anyone's guess what it really is.

Still, it's not at all impossible that some big cats have been roaming freely across the British countryside. Some suggest that a number of big cats may have been released into the wild following the 1976 Dangerous Wild Animals Act, which made it illegal to keep wild animals as pets. But is it really possible that any of these animals would have successfully reproduced and that their offspring would still be thriving today? The jury is out. Some of the sightings have turned out to be deliberate hoaxes (a cuddly tiger placed in a field, a fuzzy photo of a panther cardboard cut-out) and many others may simply be misidentifications caused by poor perspective or a trick of the light. Plenty of evidence has been found – paw prints, droppings, the carcasses of prey and even scratch marks on trees – but none of it has yet proved absolutely conclusive.

Teddy the Essex lion

A Maine Coon cat called Teddy Bear was briefly known as the Lion of Essex after a member of the public took a photograph of what appeared to be an unusually large cat in a field in St Osyth, near Clacton-on-Sea. Witnesses said that the cat, with a beige body and a white chest, was 'just preening itself'. One local resident even thought they may have heard a loud roar. Specially trained armed officers were sent to the scene, just in case. The following day, Teddy Bear's owner came forward to say her cat regularly prowled around the fields where the 'lion' was spotted and she believed he fitted the description of the cat captured on film.

Buttered up

It used to be said that the best way to stop a cat wandering away from a new home is to put butter on their paws before letting them out. One reason put forward for this dubious piece of folk advice is that the cat will immediately lick their paws, picking up the scent of the new home at the same time. Another explanation is that the process of licking reduces stress. In fact, shoving your cat's paws in the butter dish is more likely to make them stressed, and cats don't need to lick their paws to know they're somewhere unfamiliar.

Butter on a cat's paws is an old idea that still has some currency and many of us will recognise this belief, even if we doubt how well it would actually work in practice. A number of even more bizarre ideas have long been forgotten. One suggestion for settling a cat into a new home was to put puss through a window backwards. Another idea was to place the cat inside the oven (while it was cold) for a while. There's no sensible explanation for why anyone would think that either of these strategies would work, but at least it's better than the belief, widely held in Ireland, that it was unlucky to even think of taking a cat with you should you move.

COMPOSER'S COMPANION

The cat plays musical muse

Cats are often completely silent, but they do have an extensive vocal repertoire, although the noises they make can be less than harmonious, to say the least. The shrieking and caterwauling of mating cats, in particular, has disturbed the slumber of even the soundest sleeper, often in the very dead of night. Yet cats also produce a number of sounds that are extremely pleasing, even soothing, to the human ear and they do a good line in plaintive mewling and voluptuous purrs. Cats not only make their own sweet music, they also inspire human composers to take to the musical score. Many musicians have been drawn to cats and a few have even encouraged their cats to compose their own tunes.

Fiddlesticks

The nursery rhyme about the cat and the fiddle, the acrobatic cow, the laughing dog and an unlikely romance between a dish and a spoon is an amusing piece of nonsense of unknown origin. Cats, of course, would struggle with the finger movements required to play the violin (just as even the most athletic cow would never make it over the moon). The fact that this popular rhyme obviously doesn't make any sense has led to a long tradition of wild speculation about the supposedly hidden meanings behind the ditty. One interpretation involves complex comings and goings between lovers at the Elizabethan court, another turns to the ancient world for illumination, and yet one more explains the rhyme in terms of the constellations. There are many more theories, generally based on weak evidence, and one or two that are almost certainly deliberate hoaxes.

There is no record of the nursery rhyme before around 1765, so an ancient origin is unlikely. Intriguingly though, there were inns called The Cat and the Fiddle much earlier, so that part of the rhyme may have a bit of history behind it. It could possibly be a reference to Catherine of Aragon, the first wife of Henry VIII, who was also known as Catherine La Fidèle. A number of other people known as La Fidèle have also been suggested (again, with somewhat flimsy evidence). Disappointingly, the most unlikely explanation of all is that there was once a real cat who could actually play the fiddle.

Rattle and shake

The ancient Egyptians turned their adoration of cats into a fine art. Their musical abilities, however, may have lacked a certain finesse, if their musical instruments are anything to go by. A popular instrument was a type of rattle called a sistrum – a metal hoop on a handle which had movable rods attached to it. When shaken, it would have made quite a racket. This noisy instrument had sacred significance and was most commonly associated with the goddess Bastet, who usually appeared in the form of a cat. Figures of Bastet often show her holding a sistrum, and there are figures of cats attached onto many sistrums. Both cats and sistrums were central to religious ceremonies, so it's not surprising they shared symbolic space. Still, it's hard to believe that real cats would have been much impressed by the din that Bastet's instrument of choice must have made.

Calm and composed

It's not especially surprising that many classical composers have shared their homes with cats. More unexpected, perhaps, is that cats have been represented in music quite a few times, and by composers of considerable note. Prokofiev made a cat dance in his ballet *Cinderella*, and turned a clarinet into a cat in *Peter and the Wolf*, a piece of music which has introduced the orchestra to generations of young people. Tchaikovsky created music for *Puss in Boots* and *The White Cat*, Stravinsky wrote a cycle of cat lullabies and Rossini's comic song 'The Cats' Duet' has two sopranos spitting meows at each other. Ravel (who had Siamese cats) composed an opera, *L'Enfant et les Sortilèges*, which features cat characters and is based on a short story by the cat-loving French writer Colette.

Cats have not only inspired music, they have even had a go at composing it. Chopin's 'Cat Waltz' was apparently inspired by a cat running across the composer's piano. Scarlatti's 'Cat's Fugue' (more properly, but less appealingly, known as 'Fugue in G Minor') was said to be the work of his cat, Pulcinella, who was fond of scampering on the composer's harpsichord. Scarlatti may have helped a little, of course.

Musical chairs

The Russian composer Alexander Borodin spent his life surrounded by cats. Friend and fellow composer Nikolai Rimsky-Korsakov describes a visit to the Borodin household in his autobiography. Cats, he says, would sit around the composer's neck, made use of all the furniture and were free to wander across the dining table at meal times, while Borodin and his wife, Yekatyerina, related each cat's personal history.

Second-hand gossip

Johannes Brahms may be regarded as one of the greatest composers of his age, but he has a very unfortunate reputation when it comes to cats. Rumour has it that he would shoot at cats from a window in his Vienna apartment using a bow and arrow. To add insult to injury, he would then reel them inside on a line and turn their dying cries into music. This, at least, is the story that has been doing the rounds for a long while now and still gets repeated to this day. It turns out, however, that Brahms is probably not guilty as charged. There are a number of gaping holes in the accounts of Brahms' supposed cat slaying and no first-hand evidence whatsoever.

The most likely explanation for how this horrible story got off the ground is professional rivalry. The War of the Romantics is a conflict that has passed many of us by, but this aesthetic schism caused a storm in the world of classical music during the latter part of the 19th century. Brahms was of the old, traditional school and, therefore, much detested by modernisers, including fellow German composer Richard Wagner. More recent research suggests that it was Wagner (rarely generous to his rivals) who spread the cat-killing rumour to besmirch an entirely innocent Brahms.

Pulling strings

The katzenklavier, or cat organ, is a very unusual instrument indeed. Several little boxes are attached to a keyboard and cats are placed into each one, arranged chromatically, and their tails tied to the keys by a cord. When a key is struck, a nail is driven into the tail, causing the cat to howl. This peculiar contraption sounds extremely unpleasant (both for the cats and the listening audience) and is also almost certainly purely hypothetical. For a start, it wouldn't actually work (cats may howl in pain, but not in tune) and there is no evidence that one was ever actually made.

It does, however, exist in the ever-fertile human imagination. The organ was described in 1650 in a book about bizarre inventions and was said to have been used to amuse the king of Spain or possibly an Italian prince. A number of descriptions and illustrations of such an organ have appeared over the centuries, including one account about how a cat organ could be used to treat psychiatric patients. All of these descriptions seem to be conceptual rather than actual and probably say a lot more about our sense of the absurd than our treatment of cats.

Cats' chorus

Of all the ways to make a living, training cats to make music is not near the top of anyone's list; it's probably not even at the bottom. But Samuel Bisset must have thought it was worth a go when he opened Bisset's Cats' Opera at London's Haymarket Theatre in 1758. The show, which featured supposedly singing cats plucking at stringed instruments, as well as a dancing monkey, was briefly a great success. But, perhaps not surprisingly, the novelty soon wore off and Bisset apparently took to training birds to spell people's names.

Strike a chord

If cats have access to a piano at home, chances are they will jump on it, rub against it, walk along it and maybe even tap out a few notes. Many cats do seem intrigued by the sounds pianos make and may amuse themselves by pawing at the keys. For one cat, this musical ability has led to international recognition. An American cat called Nora performed via video link with the Klaipeda Chamber Orchestra under the baton of Lithuanian conductor, Mindaugas Piečaitis. The work, called *CATcerto*, was composed by the conductor and inspired by Nora's internet piano performances. Her contribution was, it has to be said, a little avant garde and involved some unconventional face-rubbing manoeuvres, but it was warmly received by the audience. The four-minute piece has been performed at numerous concert halls round the world since its premiere in 2009.

KITIONARY CORNER

Cat, n. /kæt/

The slang sense of the word 'cat' to mean a man (similar to 'guy') emerged in the African-American community during the 1920s. A narrower meaning, denoting a jazz enthusiast, was first recorded in 1931.

TEN SONGS FOR CATS TO SING ALONG TO...

Mean Eyed Cat (1960): Johnny Cash

What's New Pussycat? (1965): Tom Jones

The Cat in the Window (1967): Petula Clark

Honky Cat (1972): Elton John

Year of the Cat (1976): Al Stewart

Cool for Cats (1979): Squeeze

Cat People (1982): David Bowie

Stray Cat Strut (1982): The Stray Cats

The Love Cats (1983): The Cure

Black Cat (1990): Black Cat

...AND ONE WHERE A CAT PLAYS SECOND FIDDLE

The old music hall favourite 'Daddy Wouldn't Buy Me a Bow-Wow' was first sung in 1892 by Vesta Victoria, who held a kitten throughout the number. 'I've got a little cat,' she sang, 'and I'm very fond of that,' but what she really wanted, of course, was a dog.

THE CAT IN WORDS

From pen to paper and turn of phrase

Cats don't have much use for words (although they can be surprisingly articulate when they want to be), but human language is peppered with phrases and proverbs inspired by our feline companions. Cats have played a small part in literature down the ages and sometimes even played a pivotal role in fiction. They've certainly sat on the laps of many writers, who often appreciate a cat's company (even if they do sometimes try to sit on the page and have probably knocked over an inkpot or two). Cats can be soothing and inspiring, or simply introduce a welcome distraction into the writer's working day. Many writers have had close relationships with their feline friends and this bond has often been reflected on the page.

In my name

The word the ancient Egyptians used for 'cat' was something like 'miw', most likely an onomatopoeic representation of the sound cats make. The word 'cat', or something very much like it, is nearly universal across European languages, suggesting an ancient origin, although its precise beginnings are obscure. The Latin word *felis* (which gives us 'feline') seems to have given way to *cattus* in the Roman world, around the fourth or fifth century. One theory is that *kaddiska*, the word thought to have been used by the Berbers of North Africa (home to some of the earliest domesticated cats), slowly seeped into other languages and morphed into 'cat' and its variants.

KITIONARY CORNER

Kitty, n. /ˈkɪ.ti/

A pool of money which a group of people contribute to for a shared purpose. The term has nothing to do with cats and is probably derived from the word 'kit' (meaning a set of parts). First recorded in the 1800s, it originally described a pot of money used for a card game.

How to say 'cat' in ten languages

Go almost anywhere in Europe and you'll have a fair chance of making yourself understood if you say 'cat' (although in some languages the initial 'c' is replaced with a 'g'). Some other languages around the world use a word that sounds like the noise people make when they're trying to attract a cat's attention (something like 'puss') or they represent the sound cats themselves make (something like 'meow'). Here are ten languages where the word for 'cat' is basically 'cat'.

Chat (French)

Gatto (Italian)

Kot (Polish)

Gato (Portuguese)

Kat (Dutch)

Katze (German)

Köttur (Icelandic)

Katė (Lithuanian)

Qattus (Maltese)

Cath (Welsh)

The cat will mew

William Shakespeare was not a massive cat fan. At least that's the impression you might get from the forty or so references to cats in his plays. This is very much a sign of the times, as cats were not held in very high esteem in the Elizabethan age. This is underlined when Benedick in *Much Ado about Nothing* makes a casual quip about the contemporary practice of violence towards cats ('Hang me in a bottle like a cat and shoot me'). When applied to a human, the term 'cat' was often an insult. Tybalt in *Romeo and Juliet* is disdainfully described as 'king of cats' and, when Lysander calls Hermia a cat in *Midsummer Night's Dream*, it is not a compliment, but rather a reference to what he sees as her wayward sexuality. There's perhaps a sneaking respect for the cat in *Henry IV, Part I*, ('I am as vigilant as a cat to steal cream'), but the best thing to be said of a cat in *The Merchant of Venice* is that it is 'a harmless necessary cat', which falls somewhat short of high praise.

For future reference

Dr Samuel Johnson had a lot to say about words. He was a writer, editor, essayist, literary critic, poet and biographer, and he became one of the most important men of letters of his age. His most lasting legacy was *A Dictionary of the English Language*, which was first published in 1755. This wasn't the first dictionary of English, but it became one of the most influential accounts of contemporary English usage. Johnson's entry for cat reads: 'A domestic animal that catches mice, commonly reckoned by naturalists the lowest order of the leonine species. 'This description may not give the impression that Johnson was much taken by the species, but in fact he was very fond of cats, particularly his cat Hodge, who was said to have been greatly indulged. The cat was fed on oysters (which Johnson purchased himself) and was described by his owner as 'a very fine cat, a very fine cat indeed'.

These boots are made for walking

'Puss in Boots' is one of the best-known fairy stories to feature a cat in the starring role. The tale tells of a youngest son who inherits nothing more than a cat from his poor father. The clever feline asks to be furnished with a bag and a pair of boots and then proceeds to use cunning to bring about a dramatic reversal in his master's fortunes. The magical animal who helps a usually humble person to make good in the world is a common theme linking folktales from around the world and across the centuries; 'Puss in Boots' was just one incarnation of a long tradition. It first appeared in written form in Italy during the 16th century, but became most famous when it was written up towards the end of the 17th century by the French author Charles Perrault, who re-told a lot of the fairy tales that we still love today (including 'Little Red Riding Hood' and 'Cinderella'). Perrault published a collection of fairy tales in the 1690s which included the story of Puss in Boots. At the time, this quick-witted, intelligent cat hero represented a break with the past, which had put much darker, demonic felines at the heart of folk legend. The tremendous success of the stories across Europe can even be said to have played a part in restoring the reputation of the much-maligned cat.

KITIONARY CORNER

Catwalk, n. /ˈkatwɔːk/

First recorded in the 1880s, 'catwalk' is used to mean a long, narrow walkway, originally on ships or backstage at theatres. The term is a reference to the way cats nimbly navigate the narrowest of paths. Used to describe a platform for fashion models to walk along since the 1940s.

Rhyme and reason

The letter 'c' on a nursery alphabet frieze is often represented by a cat and, as we all know, the cat sat on the mat. If you come to think about it, cats are with us on our first tentative steps towards words and rhyme. This word association can last a lifetime and many poets have been besotted with cats. Algernon Charles Swinburne opens his poem 'To a Cat' with, 'Stately, kindly, lordly friend', which may seem a bit over the top, even to a true cat devotee. W. B. Yeats was driven to mystical contemplation in 'The Cat and the Moon', which describes a cat performing a lunar dance. The 18th-century poet Christopher Smart detected a hint of the sublime in his cat, Jeoffry, who was described as a 'servant of the living God' in a long poem called 'For I Will Consider My Cat Jeoffry'. From William Wordsworth to Ted Hughes, many of our best-loved poets have written poems about cats, enough to fill a number of anthologies of feline verse. The perfect book to curl up together with.

Practically speaking

The most famous collection of cat verse must be T. S. Eliot's Old Possum's Book of Practical Cats. Arguably the most significant poet of the 20th century, Eliot was born in America, but settled in Britain as a young man in 1914. Otherwise known for his innovative, modernist poems, which can be a bit of challenge to read, Eliot found a moment to pen a lighter work in 1939. The practical cats hold down a number of jobs, from actor to conjurer to railway worker. There's even a master criminal, Macavity the mystery cat. Eliot was a genuine ailurophile (a person who loves cats) and had quite a number of pet cats, all with amusing names such as Wiscus and Pettipaws. His close observations of real cats are apparent in his practical cats, which exhibit some of the feline characteristics we all recognise: stealth, agility, vanity, laziness and mystery. Eliot's work, although successful in its own right, went stratospheric in 1981 when Andrew Lloyd Webber turned the poems into a West End stage musical, simply called *Cats*. Most of the songs in the show are faithful to the original text and *Cats* has brought Rum Tum Tugger, Mungojerrie and Rumpelteazer to the attention of a whole new audience.

Don't bother with a lead

Rudyard Kipling's *Just So Stories* are a series of tales for children which provide imaginative explanations for how animals got to be the way they are. Thus we learn why the camel got the hump and how leopards earned their spots. 'The Cat that Walked by Himself' tells the story of how wild Man is tamed by his encounter with Woman. They move into a cosy cave together and set up home. The wild animals round about are all curious about this new way of living. First, the Wild Dog approaches the cave and soon becomes First Friend. Then the Wild Horse and the Wild Cow turn themselves in for domestication. All the while, the cat clings on to independence and refuses to go into the cave. Eventually, the cat relents and takes up a place in front of the fire in return for catching mice and making friends with the baby. But still the cat insists, 'I am the Cat that walks by himself' and pops off into the night. As it happens, this sweet little bedtime story is a surprisingly accurate description of how cat domestication probably occurred. Kipling's cat, rather like real cats, is only partly tamed and will forever have a wild side.

Cheesy grin

The heroine of Lewis Carroll's *Alice's Adventures in Wonderland* has a pet cat called Dinah who catches mice and enjoys a saucer of milk. What she doesn't do is grin. Nor do parts of her body fade in and out, and she certainly can't make herself disappear altogether. That's why Alice doesn't know what to make of the Cheshire Cat, who is a cat like no other she's encountered before. This shape-shifting cat with an enigmatic smile and a gift for sharp one-liners was the creation of Charles Lutwidge Dodgson, an Oxford lecturer in mathematics who wrote under the pen name Lewis Carroll in his spare time.

Dodgson clearly had a vivid imagination, but some of his most memorable characters were actually inspired by popular idioms of the day. The March Hare and the Mad Hatter are two examples, as is the Cheshire Cat. The origin of the expression 'grinning like a Cheshire cat' pre-dates Alice's trip down the rabbit hole, although we don't know exactly when or where it comes from. One theory is that the phrase refers to the work of a Cheshire pub-sign painter who wasn't very good at painting lions. Another suggestion links the Cheshire cat to that county's famous cheese.

American gothic

There's nothing particularly original about putting a black cat in a horror story, but Edgar Allan Poe was the master of the genre and his short story 'The Black Cat' still sends a chill down the spine. The cat in question, as you might expect, has a terrible time of it. The story describes a man's descent into alcoholism and violence, first against a pet cat called Pluto, then against his wife. The spirit of Pluto haunts the narrator, who is finally exposed for his crimes. Although the cat suffers during the course of the story, there is no sense that this brutality is deserved. Pluto is very definitely the innocent party and all the guilt and demonic possession belongs to the human narrator.

Poe himself adored cats and they provided much comfort in what was often a tormented and difficult life. He often worked with his tortoiseshell cat, Catarina, perched on his shoulders. Poe (much like his ill-fated narrator) had problems with alcohol and money, which can't have been easy for his very young wife, Virginia, who developed tuberculosis when only in her teens. One visitor to the Poe household noted that, in the absence of money for heating, Virginia's only source of warmth was her husband's coat and the family cat. Black cats have often been presented in myth and fiction as malevolent creatures of ill-intent, but Poe does something different in 'The Black Cat'. Feline retribution, yes; ghastly revenge, of course. But the reader is on the side of the cat all the way.

Farewell to arms (hello to toes)

The great American novelist Ernest Hemingway is well known for his tough characters and big themes of war and courage. Generally regarded as a bit of a macho character, he also had a soft side. It seems the author couldn't resist cats and he shared his home in Key West, Florida, with around fifty at any one time and also kept cats at his winter residence in Cuba. He wrote affectionately about his cats in his letters and seems to have taken a great interest in them, even teaching them tricks. Hemingway is best known for keeping polydactyl cats (which have six or more toes); indeed, this type of cat is sometimes known as a Hemingway cat. The writer was given a six-toed cat by a sailor and he subsequently became a fan. As the trait is passed on genetically, he soon had a clutch of them. After his death in 1961, his house in Key West became a museum. There are still around forty to fifty polydactyl cats in residence.

Ten Writers who loved cats

Cats and writers make perfect companions. Cats are not generally as demanding as dogs, but they still provide valuable companionship for those who often work at home and alone. The list of writers who have loved, adored and been inspired by their feline friends is a long one and goes back a long way. Here are just ten writers who doted on cats.

Lord Byron: The flamboyant Romantic poet scandalised polite society with his romantic escapades and unconventional tastes. He was no less groundbreaking when it came to his choice of pets. He famously kept a bear while studying at Cambridge and later owned peacocks, monkeys, a falcon and a crow. Known for his utter devotion to his Newfoundland dog, Boatswain, Byron also had several cats, including one who reputedly drank milk from a skull, although this detail may be a poetic embellishment to enhance an already colourful reputation.

Walter Scott: The Scottish novelist and poet was one of the most popular writers of his day and was a great lover of animals. He kept a number of dogs, but it was his tomcat, Hinse, who was said to rule the roost and would think nothing of taking a swipe at an impertinent hound. In one portrait of the author at work, a dog sits on the floor, while Hinse lies on top of the desk. Scott once described cats as mysterious creatures: 'There's more passing in their minds than we are aware of.'

The Brontë sisters: Charlotte, Emily and Anne, the three sisters who became one of the most remarkable literary families in English literature, lived an outwardly quiet life at their father's parsonage in Haworth, West Yorkshire. They shared their home with numerous pets, which provided the young women with entertainment, companionship and also sadness at their passing. All of this was recorded in letters and diaries, and cats make occasional appearances in the novels. Emily wrote an essay about cats, in which she says, 'I can say with sincerity that I like cats; also I can give very good reasons why those who despise them are wrong.'

Charles Baudelaire: The French poet led the life of a tortured artist to perfection. He was eccentric, decadent, hopeless with money and dabbled in drugs. He also loved cats. In fact, it was said that he would pay far more attention to a cat than to any humans in the room. He became notorious for his collection of poems *Les Fleurs de Mal*, which was published in 1857 and explored the themes of sex and death. It included three poems about cats, which are largely symbolic and characterised as embodying female qualities.

Charles Dickens: The great novelist explored all aspects of Victorian society, from the top to the bottom, from the light to the dark. There are cats in a number of his novels, which similarly reflect the highs and lows of feline existence at the time, from pampered companions to ill-treated strays. Dickens also wrote compassionately about the plight of London's strays in his non-fiction writing. There were real cats in Dickens' life too. One cat, called William, had to be quickly renamed Williamina when a litter of kittens arrived.

Edward Lear: The writer of delightful nonsense verse who gave the world the humorous poem 'The Owl and the Pussycat' had one particularly cherished companion, his tabby cat, Foss. The cat was often featured in Lear's verses and drawings, which included a series of Foss in comically heraldic poses. Foss, who arrived in the Lear household as a kitten, was rotund and only had half a tail. The Lear family moved to San Remo in Italy in the 1870s, where first Foss then Lear died within months of each other.

Alexandre Dumas: The French novelist who wrote *The Three Musketeers* and *The Count of Monte Cristo* had many pet cats, including Mysouff, who supposedly had telepathic powers. Dumas was convinced that his cat knew when he was coming home, even if he was thrown off his normal schedule. Mysouff's successor, Mysouff II, was said to have enlisted the help of the family's pet monkeys in order to break into the cage housing

Dumas' collection of exotic birds. Dumas joined together with a number of other writers to befriend the stray cats of Paris.

Mark Twain: The American author of *The Adventures of Tom Sawyer* was a life-long cat lover who kept a number of them at his Connecticut farm and loved to have them round about him while he worked. They were given elaborate names, such as Apollinaris, Beelzebub, Blatherskite and Zoroaster. The reason, he said, was to help teach his children how to grapple with difficult words. Twain is famous for his witty aphorisms and came up with some great lines about cats. 'If man could be crossed with a cat,' goes one, 'it would improve man but deteriorate the cat.'

Colette: Few writers are so closely associated with cats as the French novelist Colette. The author had a colourful career in music hall theatre, got through three husbands and spent her whole life surrounded by cats and dogs. Her cats had fanciful names like Fanchette, La Touteu and Petiteu, and she came up with great quotes, such as 'Time spent with cats is never wasted.' Her novella *The Cat* describes a curious ménage à trois between a man who is besotted with his cat, Saha, and his fiancée, Camille, who is not so impressed by her feline rival.

Doris Lessing: Famous for serious and groundbreaking novels such as *The Grass is Singing* and *The Golden Notebook*, Lessing was a formidable figure in 20th-century literature and was a Nobel Prize winner in 2007. Among her many literary accomplishments are a number of books about cats. She was first intrigued by cats while growing up on an African farm. Later, she shared her London home with a number of cats and wrote fondly and perceptively about them. Her last cat book was called *The Old Age of El Magnifico*, which describes the declining years of a lovable cat.

While the cat's away

Cats crop up rather a lot in many familiar proverbs, and not always in flattering ways. They are proverbially portrayed as killjoy tyrants ('while the cat's away the mice will play'), as troublemakers ('put the cat among the pigeons'), as smug ('the cat that got the cream') or as arrogant creatures who don't know their place ('the cat may look at a king'). If that isn't bad enough, they are criminally cunning ('cat burglar'), recklessly inquisitive ('curiosity killed the cat') and have dubious sexual practices ('cathouse'). On top of that, they are subjected to violence in everyday phrases ('there's more than one way to skin a cat' or 'there are more ways of killing a cat than choking it with cream'). A 'cat's chance', of course, is no chance at all.

The source of such colourful phrases is invariably obscure. Interesting theories are often put forward, but they don't always stand up to closer inspection. The phrase which describes a small space, 'not enough room to swing a cat', for example, is often said to be short-hand for the cat o' nine tails, a knotted whip once used to punish sailors. Written records, however, suggest that the proverb is older than the punishment, throwing that theory into the water. Of course, it might be true, but watertight evidence is hard to come by.

'To let the cat out of the bag' (meaning to reveal a secret) is similarly hard to pin down. It may refer to dodgy practices at country fairs, when cats were fraudulently sold in place of something more edible. Again, though, there's no hard evidence for this theory. It seems a little incredible that practical country folk would have had the wool pulled over their eyes quite so easily; farmers are not that likely to have bought livestock sight unseen. What we do know, however, is that the phrase has been used with its proverbial meaning since the 1760s.

Take an umbrella

The expression 'it's raining cats and dogs' certainly captures the imagination and has prompted quite a lot of speculation about its origin. It has been rather poetically explained as a reference to Norse mythology, which supposedly associated cats and dogs with the weather. Needless to say, there's not a shred of evidence for this connection. Another often repeated explanation is that it refers to the bodies of dead cats and dogs being washed along flooded city streets during very heavy rain, presumably because of inadequate drainage.

This has a ring of plausibility about it, but again, there's no hard and fast evidence that this is the origin of the saying. The strongest link comes from the author and satirist Jonathan Swift. There are 'drowned puppies' and 'dead cats' which 'come tumbling down the flood', in his satirical poem 'A Description of a City Shower', written in 1710, which could be either descriptive or hyperbolic. Swift uses the actual phrase 'rain cats and dogs' in another satire published in 1738, but we're not sure whether he was coining a phrase or repeating a cliché.

Perhaps we are guilty of being too literal when it comes to trying to interpret these linguistic snippets. It's possible that people were just playing with language and exaggerating for effect. Indeed, there are related expressions in a number of other languages. It rains chair legs in Greek, wheelbarrows in Czech and old ladies and sticks in Welsh. In Denmark shoemakers' apprentices fall from the sky, while in Columbia it is husbands that rain down. No one tries to explain these expressions with reference to facts; we just accept that humans can be very creative with words.

The bee's knees

The 'cat's whiskers' are the absolute top and as good as it gets, something they have in common with the 'gnat's elbow', the 'flea's eyebrow' and the 'elephant's wrist.' These amusing little slang terms took off in the 1920s in America and were briefly fashionable among the flapper set. The bee's knees, incidentally, is much older. First recorded in the 18th century, the phrase used to mean something tiny and insignificant. Whether the bee's knees started this verbal jesting craze or was simply resurrected in the wake of the cat's pyjamas, we'll never know.

TEN CAT PUB NAMES

Unless you count lions (especially red ones) cats don't feature much in pub names. Grouse and pheasant are not uncommon, there are lots of hounds, horses and cows and plenty of foxes and hares. A cat inn, by contrast, is a fairly rare find, and all the more satisfying for that. Here are ten pub names that appear on at least one public house somewhere in the British Isles.

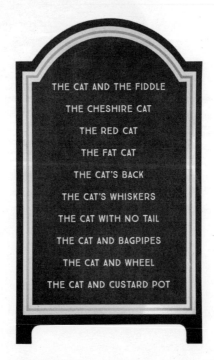

THE CAT AND THE FIDDLE

THE CHESHIRE CAT

THE RED CAT

THE FAT CAT

THE CAT'S BACK

THE CAT'S WHISKERS

THE CAT WITH NO TAIL

THE CAT AND BAGPIPES

THE CAT AND WHEEL

THE CAT AND CUSTARD POT

Toying with each other

Cats can often look as if they are deep in thought and they are certainly pleasant companions to have in quiet moments of contemplation. If you're philosophically minded, a cat might even lead you to more profound thinking. This is what happened to Michel de Montaigne, the influential French essayist of the Renaissance. With a humane attitude to animals which was well ahead of his time, Montaigne questioned the received wisdom that humans were automatically superior to animals. Playing with his cat one day, he wondered, 'When I play with my cat, who knows if I am not a pastime to her more than she is to me?'

THE CAT IN PICTURES

From oil painting to screen star

From Egyptian wall art to CGI, cats have always had their place in the visual arts. Often connected to spiritual beliefs in the ancient world, cats continued to have a symbolic significance in art well into the Renaissance. While generally left out of the family portrait, the aesthetic appeal of cats has often inspired artists. Frequently found on the canvas, cats have also been a firm favourite with cartoonists and animators, and cinema has given us some memorable cat characters. The era of the instant image has made citizen artists of us all and cats are the animal stars of the internet age. There is no better way to waste time than uploading or downloading videos of cats doing the cutest, funniest things.

That's me in the picture

The celebrated art historian Kenneth Clark once suggested that there were few cats in portraits because their owners lacked pride in their feline companions. It's true that dogs, horses or even cattle are more likely to grace a grand person's portrait than a humble cat. These animals say something about the owner's status in a way a cat never could. The fact that it's quite hard to get a cat to sit still on demand may also be a factor, but there's no denying that cats are largely absent from the formal portrait.

This historic absence of the feline sitter makes one particular portrait all the more striking. Henry Wriothesley, the third Earl of Southampton, was a favourite of Queen Elizabeth I and a patron of Shakespeare. Following one of many escapades and intrigues, Southampton was imprisoned in the Tower of London for treason. Two years later, his portrait was painted by John de Critz to mark the end of his imprisonment (he was rehabilitated in 1603 under James I and became a Knight of the Garter). It's a fairly typical portrait of the Tudor age: big collars, long hair and a fancy pair of gloves. But this portrait has one very unusual feature – there is a black and white cat on the windowsill, not centre stage, but still very prominent.

There's speculation that Southampton had befriended a cat while in prison or that his wife had left the cat with him on a prison visit. The cat has even acquired a name: Trixie. Whether any of this is true or not is anyone's guess; we don't even know if the cat was real (although it does look more like an actual cat than a symbolically stylised one). Possibly the artist added the cat to underline the prisoner's isolation (with only a cat for company) or it could be a reference to contemporary superstitions, symbolising Southampton's bad luck. The cat could, of course, have been Southampton's best friend, but we'll never know for sure.

Life in a goldfish bowl

It's not only modern celebrities who live in the dazzling glare of mass media. Hanging on the wall of the National Portrait Gallery in London is a painting of a pale-skinned, pink-cheeked young woman dressed in jewels and delicate fabrics. At her elbow sits a glass bowl full of goldfish. Dangling over the side of the bowl, apparently trying to climb in, is a little black and white cat. Painted in 1765, this is the portrait of Catherine 'Kitty' Fisher, who was a well-known courtesan of some notoriety. She carefully honed her public image and became famous for being famous in a way that has become very familiar to us today. The cat in the painting (a kitten fishing) alludes to Kitty Fisher's name and the crowds of people seen reflected in the goldfish bowl symbolise the public attention that Fisher attracted during her life.

Angels and demons

Diabolic felines can be found in the stonework on churches across Western Europe, right alongside gargoyles of demons and fiends. These cats symbolised the superstitions of the medieval age, but the Renaissance represented the cat in a different light. Although cats don't get a mention in the Bible, they began appearing in religious paintings during the 15th and 16th centuries, no doubt to add layers of meaning. The cat was sometimes evil, often ambivalent and occasionally even good.

Cats appear from time to time in scenes of biblical births. Leonardo da Vinci, no less, created a series of sketches of the *Madonna and Child* in the 1470s which show the infant Jesus clutching a cat. A later example is Barocci's painting The Madonna of the Cat, a depiction of the Holy Family painted around 1575, which shows Mary, Joseph, John the Baptist and the infant Jesus in a relaxed and informal mood. The infant John the Baptist teases a cat with his foot. The cats in these scenes look like perfectly ordinary family pets, but cats often appear as a malevolent presence in other examples of religious art. A number of artists of the period produced paintings of the Last Supper in which a cat sits at the feet of Judas. The presence of these cats hints at the betrayal to come and symbolises the devil's presence.

TEN ARTISTS WHO PUT CATS IN THE PICTURE

Leonardo da Vinci: The Italian polymath was one of the greatest artists who has ever lived, but he often didn't get round to finishing things. Still, even a page of doodles from a genius is quite something. In 1513, da Vinci produced a page of wonderful cat sketches. Being an anatomist as well as an artist, he was fascinated by form and movement, and his drawings perfectly capture the essence of the cat in both naturalist and fantastical form. Some of the sketches are utterly realistic and show cats having a nap or a wash, while others are more stylised depictions of the cat form.

William Hogarth: The 18th-century painter, engraver and satirist was horrified by animal cruelty. An image of cats being abused features in the first part of his series of prints *The Four Stages of Cruelty*, linking inhumanity to animals with a lack of compassion for fellow humans. Hogarth also painted portraits and one in particular includes a very cheeky cat. *The Graham Children* shows the offspring of Daniel Graham, who was apothecary to the king. A cat has clawed its way up the back of a chair. Not far off is a bird in a cage.

Utagawa Kuniyoshi:

A master of the distinctive Japanese art of woodcut prints, Kuniyoshi often put cats in his work. Sometimes they were the mythical animals of Japanese legend, such as one which shows a samurai warrior grappling with a monstrous feline. Others depict more domestic scenes, in which elegantly dressed women, often geishas, recline gracefully with a cat at their side. Kuniyoshi also used anthropomorphic images of cats to parody social foibles. His cats wear kimonos and serve tea, all the while managing to be both convincingly feline and recognisably human.

Edouard Manet:

The French impressionist painter caused shock and scandal when his nude portrait Olympia went on display in Paris in 1865. It wasn't so much the nudity (there was nothing unusual about nakedness in art) as the bold allusions to prostitution which upset genteel gallery-goers of the time. The small black cat which stands on the end of Olympia's bed, all arched back and raised tail, would have been widely understood as a symbol of sexuality. As well as symbolic felines, Manet also included companion cats in many of his paintings, and his own cat, Zizi, makes a number of appearances on the canvas.

Pierre-Auguste Renoir:

In contrast to many other artists over the ages, this French artist rarely used the cat as a symbolic device. Very much a cat person, Renoir's felines are very clearly cherished family pets. While his cats add a touch of sensuality to portraits, they are naturalistically portrayed, often clasped fondly in a girl's embrace or curled up contentedly on a woman's lap. One striking example is *Sleeping Girl with Cat*, a large canvas depicting a girl who has nodded off in a chair with a beautiful blue cat languorously stretched out on her lap.

Pablo Picasso: This avant-garde artist changed the way we think about art with his decidedly unconventional approach to representing the world. He created people with eyes in odd places and limbs at funny angles, and there were oddly shaped cats in his work too. Picasso had cats, as well as numerous other animal companions, and he was fascinated by their stalking, prowling, hunting prowess. He often depicted cats as worthy predators. *Cat and Crab on the Beach*, for example, shows what looks like a valiant confrontation between equals. Picasso also turned the ferocity of cats on the hunt into a representation of the horrors of the war.

Paul Klee: The Swiss-German artist was influenced by the Cubist movement and developed his own highly distinctive style. Klee had a number of cats during his lifetime, all valued family members. Klee was said to have been relaxed about cats wandering across his still-wet canvases, arguing that paw prints would give critics of the future something to wonder about. Cats often have a presence in his work as well. One example is the expressionistic *Cat and Bird*, in which a cat's head fills the entire frame. Another similarly close-up cat portrait is wittily entitled *Idol for House Cats*.

David Hockney: The Yorkshire-born artist has used a wide range of techniques and styles throughout his long career and touched on many different themes. During the 1960s and 70s he produced a series of portraits, including the well-known work *Mr and Mrs Clark and Percy*. The couple were the designers Ossie Clark and Celia Birtwell (friends of the artist) and Percy was one of their cats. Sitting upright on Ossie's lap, Percy represents the free-spirited milieu which the designers inhabited. The cat is also a humorous reference to the many classical paintings of couples where a dog is used to represent fidelity.

Andy Warhol: The American pop artist best known for his soup cans and colourful celebrity prints was a big fan of cats. All his cats were called Sam (expect one, which was called Hester) and in 1954 he printed a limited edition, hand-coloured book of lithographs entitled *25 Cats Name Sam and One Blue Pussy*. The calligraphy was done by the artist's cat-loving mother, Julia (who was also responsible for the grammatical error in the title, which Warhol decided to keep). There were actually only sixteen illustrations of cats named Sam (and one blue cat).

Tracey Emin: One of a number of artists widely credited with having shaken up the British art world in the 1980s, Emin is one of the most critically and commercially successful artists working today. No wonder then that when her cat, Docket, disappeared in 2002, the 'missing' posters she put up were quickly taken down, presumably to be added to amateur art collections. They were said to be changing hands for not inconsiderable sums of money. Happily, Docket was found a few days later. Docket has appeared several times in Emin's work and has his own collection of ceramics, all featuring cat sketches by the artist.

A life drawing cats

Lots of artists have put cats into paintings, but one man devoted his whole career to feline art. Louis Wain was born in London in 1860 and trained to be an artist. To begin with, he made a living doing illustrations of country matters (often featuring animals) for various magazines, but when he was in his twenties, cats started taking over his work. This new focus was in no small part down to Peter, a stray black and white cat adopted by the Wain family who features frequently in the artist's work.

Wain produced hundreds of cat drawings, ranging from naturalistic sketches to more experimental portraits showing close-ups of wide-eyed cats against vivid, psychedelic backdrops. His interest in cats led him to become president of the National Cat Club (the body responsible for organising pedigree cat shows and setting breed standards), although he didn't actually keep show cats. He was most famous for his humorous, anthropomorphic illustrations which depicted cats engaged in human

THE CAT IN PICTURES

activities such as attending soirées, going to the opera, playing golf and
having wheelbarrow races. These sweet, comical images were used to
illustrate dozens of children's books, magazine articles and advertisements,
and appeared on countless greetings cards and postcards.

Despite the immense popularity of his drawings, Wain was not a canny
businessman and he sold his work outright, meaning he did not receive
royalties for the many reproductions of his pictures. He was also plagued by
mental ill-health and spent much of his later life in institutions, although he
continued drawing cats even while in hospital. After his death in 1939, his
style went out of fashion and his work was largely forgotten. More recently,
however, there's been renewed interest in the cats of Louis Wain and the
original artwork is highly collectable.

Puss in boots, and other items of clothing

Beatrix Potter is perhaps most famous for her bunnies. Peter Rabbit,
Benjamin Bunny, Flopsy, Mopsy and Cotton-tail have delighted generations
of children, but there is also a place for cats in the anthropomorphic tales
of Beatrix Potter. There's Mrs Tabitha Twitchit with her kittens, Mittens,
Moppet and Tom Kitten. Mr McGregor also has a cat, who traps the
naughty bunnies under a basket, and the Tailor of Gloucester has a cat
called Simpkin, who keeps mice under teacups. Then there is the unlikely
business partnership between Tomcat, Ginger and Pickles the Terrier. Some
of these cats are basically human characters in
feline form, while others are just cats. Although
dismissed as overly sentimental by some, there's
no denying the skill in Potter's drawings, all
inspired by the real animals she observed in
and around her Lake District home.

Potter died in 1943, so it was something of
a surprise when a completely unknown Beatrix

Potter tale was discovered. A few years ago, a publisher happened across a reference to *The Tale of Kitty-in-Boots* in one of Potter's letters. Following a search of the archives at the V&A Museum in London, three manuscripts were found. It seems that Potter had started the book very early on in her career and never got round to finishing it. Sadly, there is only one colour sketch of Kitty-in-Boots, but the illustrator Quentin Blake (who worked on many of the Roald Dahl stories) will complete the drawings so the tale can finally be published, over a century after it was first began.

A cat's breakfast

The much-loved film *Breakfast at Tiffany's* stars Audrey Hepburn in one of her most enchanting performances. The romantic comedy sees Hepburn's character, New York socialite Holly Golightly, embark on a friendship with her writer neighbour, Paul Varjak. Key to the film's charm is the song 'Moon River', but let's not forget about 'Something for Cat', a wordless tune on the soundtrack. Holly may be flighty, she may be frivolous, she may be a good-time girl, but she has a cat. This keeps her grounded and loosely in touch

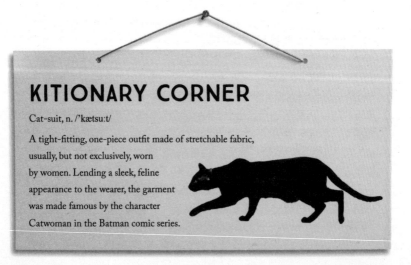

KITIONARY CORNER

Cat-suit, n. /ˈkætsuːt/

A tight-fitting, one-piece outfit made of stretchable fabric, usually, but not exclusively, worn by women. Lending a sleek, feline appearance to the wearer, the garment was made famous by the character Catwoman in the Batman comic series.

with domesticity, which ultimately redeems her. The cat (known simply as Cat in the film) was played by a feline professional called Orangey, who had a number of roles in film and television and was something of a pioneer in the cat show business world.

Voices off

The 1962 animated film *Gay Purr-ee* seems to have been almost completely forgotten. Admittedly, it's not the best film title ever, but the main character, Mewsette, was voiced by the legendary Judy Garland, so you might expect the film to be a little better known. The feline-themed cartoon tells the tale of Mewsette, a farm cat who abandons her rural home for the bright lights of Paris. Garland gave Mewsette words and music, but that wasn't enough to impress the critics and the film barely made a splash before sinking without trace.

We're with the bad guy

Although the reputation of cats has come a long way over the centuries, cinematic felines are just as likely to be creepy, scary and untrustworthy as their counterparts in folk superstitions, medieval art or 19th-century ghost stories. Horror films, of course, have made the most of the cat's spookier aspects. *The Black Cat*, starring Boris Karloff and Bela Lugosi, is a typical example of the genre. The film of Stephen King's novel *Pet Sematary* also continues a long tradition of spectral felines.

Even animated cats in perfectly sweet children's films are often up to no good. The antics of the Siamese cats in *Lady and the Tramp* are a memorable instance of feline misbehaviour. When the pair cause havoc in the home, the entirely innocent Lady gets the blame. Duchess, the Persian cat in *Babe*, the story of a talking (and singing) pig, is similarly ill-disposed towards her fellow creatures. In *Cats and Dogs* things are even worse. The entire cat population of the world seems to be involved in a plot to make all humans allergic to dogs (the dogs, of course, are all goodies). In *All Dogs Go to Heaven 2* the very devil himself turns out to be a cat.

Most famous of all cinematic bad cats has to be the fluffy white Persian that has become a trademark of Ernst Stavro Blofeld, the arch-villain of many James Bond films. Often seen being stroked in a slow and strangely menacing fashion, Blofeld's pet has spawned many spoofs and parodies, notably in the Austin Powers films, in which Dr Evil is seen stroking a hairless cat. Of course, we don't know if Blofeld's cat is actually in on all the plotting and scheming, but there is clearly guilt by association.

The spaceship cat

Science fiction presents creative people with a world of endless possibilities. As nothing is true, script writers and directors can make anything happen. Sci-fi creatures are often fantastical beasts with physical attributes and character traits unknown in the boring old real world. An interesting choice, then, to put an ordinary moggy onto a spaceship, which is exactly what happens in Ridley Scott's 1979 film *Alien*. Ginger tom Jones is the ship's cat on the spacecraft Nostromo and forms a close bond with Ellen Ripley (played by Sigourney Weaver). Jones is never anything but a normal cat, but he has a number of plot functions. Crew members are sent off to look for him (with unfortunate consequences) and Ripley talks to him when we would not otherwise know what was going on in her head. Jones is ultimately rescued by Ripley, and they spend fifty-seven years in cryostasis together, which is where things get just a little bit unrealistic.

And the award goes to... a cat

The Picture Animal Top Star of the Year (PATSY) award was started in 1939 by the American Humane Society (the same people who reassure us that no animals were harmed during the production of a film) and continued until 1986. During that time, awards were given to lots of dogs and horses, some mules and chimps, a couple of lions, a goose, a rabbit and a sea lion. A number of cats also picked up awards over the years, including a cat called Syn, who starred in the 1965 Walt Disney comedy *That Darn Cat*, and Amber, who played the title role in *The Cat From Outer Space* in 1978.

TEN CARTOON CATS

KRAZY CAT: This early and influential comic strip was created by George Herriman and first appeared in the *New York Evening Journal* in 1913. It ran until the death of the artist in 1944 and followed the exploits of the not-too-clever Krazy and a grumpy mouse called Ignatz.

FELIX THE CAT: The cat with the enormous grin came to fame in the era of the silent movie and had a touch of Charlie Chaplin about him. He starred in around 150 silent cartoons between 1921 and 1928 and became an enormous star. His image is still found on all sorts of merchandise to this day.

SYLVESTER: This Looney Tunes creation first appeared in the 1940s and went on to be one of the best-loved cartoon cats. Forever trying (and failing) to catch his nemesis, the little yellow canary Tweety, Sylvester lisped his way through many escapades that never quite went his way.

TOM: Never apart from his mouse co-star Jerry, this famous duo were the Hanna-Barbera studio's contribution to the highly competitive cartoon market of the 1940s. Pure slapstick, the cat and mouse pair were forever chasing each other, bumping into things and hitting each other over the head with mallets. Tom usually came off worse and never caught his mouse.

THE CAT IN THE HAT: This clownish cat with the trademark red and white striped hat was created with a very serious purpose in mind: to encourage children to read. First published in 1957, its creator, Dr Seuss, used rhyme, humour and amusing illustrations to engage young learners with the often surreal antics of the Cat in the Hat.

TOP CAT: Hanna-Barbera came up with a new cartoon cat for the 1960s and this time the cat was no clown. Top Cat was cool, sassy and wise-cracking. The boater-wearing feline lived among the trash cans in a New York back alley with his gang of cat friends and spent a lot of time trying to outsmart Officer Dibble.

THE ARISTOCATS: This feature-length animated film was released by Walt Disney in 1970 and tells the tale of Duchess, the posh Parisian cat who gets into a spot of bother after inheriting a fortune. Luckily, alley cat Thomas O'Malley is on hand to save the day. With its jazzy soundtrack featuring vocals by Maurice Chevalier, this is one of the most entertaining feline-themed films ever made.

CUSTARD: The pink cat was one half of a pairing which became a British TV animation classic. *Roobarb and Custard* (Roobarb was a green dog) first aired in 1974 and a total of 30 episodes were made. The cat and dog are neighbours and the stories revolve around their competitive efforts to outwit each other. Custard is more laid back than his boundlessly enthusiastic rival.

GARFIELD: The marmalade cat created by cartoonist Jim Davis was first seen in a newspaper comic strip in 1978. Garfield lives with Jon, a slightly geeky human, as well as a dog called Odie. Smart but a bit lazy, the fat cat has a great fondness for lasagne. Garfield is the most syndicated comic strip in the world, making this one of the best-known cat characters of all time.

SIMON'S CAT: This manipulative feline was created by Simon Tofield and first appeared in an online film before having his first book published in 2009. Simon's Cat (who is never actually named) has also starred in animations and comic strips. Always hungry, Simon's Cat spends most of his time trying to persuade Simon to feed him. He is also very good at clawing things. The artist was inspired by observing the behaviour of his own cats.

Click bait

The internet has opened up a world of information in a way simply unimaginable even a couple of decades ago. All the wonders (and horrors) of the world are only a click away, so what is it that we all want to see? Cats, that's what. Cats in the bath, cats wearing sunglasses, cats watching TV, cats teasing dogs, cats doing tricks, cats hissing, pouncing, hiding, sleeping and falling off things. We even love cats looking bored and grumpy. If you are worried that the instant gratification provided by the internet is leading to short attention spans, never fear. Some of these cat video compilations are up to an hour long.

Many of these clips, uploaded by ordinary cat owners, have gone viral and been shared by millions. Some of them have turned cats into celebrities and their owners into millionaires. True, we also like to share videos of all sorts of other animals doing funny or cute things, but cats have nearly broken the internet. There's no need to feel guilty about all those hours wasted watching cats battling with boxes or clawing up curtains, researchers at an American university have concluded that watching cat videos makes us feel more positive about life and boosts our energy levels. So celebrated has the whole internet cat phenomenon become that there is even an internet cat video festival held regularly in the US. Devotees gather to watch their favourite clips and awards are given to the best ones. Psychologists and media theorists have started to take a serious interest in exactly why cats are so big on the web. Until they come up with some solid data, though, we'll have to settle for the evident truth that watching cats fighting a paper bag or knocking over a Christmas tree is just really, really funny.

Boxing clever

When the American inventor and entrepreneur Thomas Edison began experimenting with moving images, he turned his camera on an unlikely subject for some of his earliest footage: boxing cats. Using a machine called a kinetograph, Edison started making films at his studio in 1893. The first short clips he produced included a recording of a man sneezing and one of a blacksmith at work. Another, made in 1894, shows two cats in harnesses and boxing gloves, apparently having a bout in the ring.

BATTERSEA CATS

London's famous home for cats (and dogs)

There's no denying that Battersea Dogs & Cats Home is much better known for looking after dogs than caring for cats. Cats didn't even get a mention until the Home officially changed its name to include cats in 2002. It comes as a surprise to many, then, that cats have actually been part of the Battersea story since way back in 1883, only a couple of decades after the Home for Lost & Starving Dogs first opened. These days, cats are very much part of the Battersea family and over 230,000 cats have been cared for by this much-loved London institution since 1860.

How it all began

Battersea's founder, Mary Tealby, first set up her Temporary Home for Lost & Starving Dogs in London's Islington in 1860. This pioneering woman was one of a growing band of campaigners who began vocally objecting to the casual cruelty and deliberate violence that was often the lot of animals during the 19th century. Yet, despite leaving such an extraordinary legacy to London's animals, Mary left very few traces of her own life and very little is known about her. We don't even have a photograph. Sadly, she died in 1865 and never got to see the new Home in Battersea (which opened at its current site in 1871). Nor did she witness the arrival of the first cats at Battersea in 1883.

Cats at Battersea

Around the time that Mary Tealby was taking in her first stray dogs, London was positively teeming with cats. They lived in people's homes as well as in warehouses, factories and docks. Their ubiquity did nothing to boost their social standing and they were often regarded as pests, little better than mice and rats. Although some cats were undoubtedly cherished companions, neglect and cruelty were all too commonplace and few people gave much thought to cat welfare. Anyone expressing concern for cats was generally regarded as a bit of an eccentric. It was a legacy from one such person which led Battersea to start taking in cats in 1883.

The new arrivals gave the Home some difficulties. Cats, unlike dogs, were not regarded as the property of an individual, so their legal status was ambiguous. In addition, the Home raised money through charges for re-homed dogs and reclaim fees for lost dogs. It was much harder to persuade people to pay to adopt a cat and strays were rarely reclaimed.

By the turn of the century, 500 cats a year were being looked after by

Battersea. Re-homing stray cats remained a challenge, but attitudes were slowly changing. As the 20th century rolled on, cats were increasingly regarded with affection, but they would have to wait until the 21st century before a name change boosted their profile at the Home, which became Battersea Dogs & Cats Home in 2002.

KITIONARY CORNER

Tortoiseshell, n. adj. /ˈtɔː.təʃ.ʃel/

First recorded to describe a cat in the 1840s, tortoiseshell cats have particoloured coats of orange, brown and black, either speckled throughout the coat or in blotches. Cats that also have white patches are often described as calico.

Battersea cats today

A state-of-the-art cattery was built at the London centre in 2010. There are eighty-three walk-in pens, each with a heated bed area, a scratching post, places to hide and sleep, as well as the usual food and water bowls and litter trays.

In addition to looking after cats until they can be reunited with their owners or found a new home, Battersea offers a number of other special services for cats. Cats that find life in the cattery particularly stressful can be offered a place in a foster home. Cats recovering from an operation or illness can also be fostered, as can pregnant females. Where possible, it's much better for kittens to grow up in a family home, where they can be well socialised.

Not all cats are cut out for the life of a pampered pet, whether by nature or upbringing, so Battersea sometimes re-homes cats to farms and stables, where they work as mousers.

Battersea cats by numbers

Battersea has three sites, employs over 350 staff and depends on around 1000 volunteers. There are around 220 cats on site across the three centres at any one time, who are all looked after by a clinic team of 39 staff, including eight vets. On average, nine cats are taken in every day. The average stay for a cat at Battersea is 27 days. Battersea aims to never turn away a cat or dog in need.

TEN VERY SPECIAL BATTERSEA CATS

Larry, Chief Mouser to the Cabinet Office of the United Kingdom: Former Battersea resident Larry moved into No. 10 Downing Street in 2011 and soon became one of the most famous felines in the country. Since taking on his role at No. 10, Larry's been busy greeting VIPs, including American President Barack Obama.

Pluto, Battersea Arts Centre theatre cat: Since stepping into the spotlight at Battersea Arts Centre back in 2007, Pluto has made his mark both on stage and behind the scenes. When the Arts Centre was seriously damaged by fire in 2015, Pluto went missing. Fortunately, he turned up a few days later completely unharmed.

Kitty and Buttons, the cat and dog who became best of friends: a tiny puppy and kitten who were being hand-reared at Battersea's Old Windsor centre became so close that they played like litter mates. When Battersea put out an online video, the adorable pair caught international attention. They are still the best of friends and are enjoying life with a family in Essex.

Shadow and Star, feline residents of Jamyang Buddhist Centre in Kennington: These feline friends enjoy life in the ultimate haven of peace and tranquility at the London centre with Tibetan monk Geshe Tashi Tsering. Star, who is now called Tara, which is Tibetan for star, and Shadow, who has also been renamed Kala, spend their days prowling the calm courtyard and making friends with visitors.

Victoria Falls: This traffic-dodging tortie landed on her feet at a London station. When a tiny kitten narrowly avoided being hit by a car outside London's Victoria Station, before falling 15 feet into a basement, her ordeal was witnessed by a caring passer by who brought her to Battersea's nearby centre. Vets were amazed that she was unharmed. Renamed Victoria Falls, she now lives in south London, where she's keeping her other eight lives intact.

Pirate and Marley, thespian cats at the Bush Theatre: While resident at Battersea, Marley and Pirate (who only has one eye) were talent-spotted by staff from the west London theatre, who were looking for mouse catchers. The cats have since expanded their skills and also play a part in greeting the public and keeping an eye on things, as well as regularly updating their Twitter feeds.

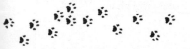

Hats off to *Bogart*, feline friend of the royal milliner: Stray cat Bogart got a sneaky peek at preparations for the Royal Wedding in 2011, when he was found wandering near the London office of famous milliner Philip Treacy. He soon found a new home with Philip Treacy's production manager, Jutta Freedlander, and Bogart enjoyed watching the special occasion from the comfort of his new home.

Orlando, Battersea's resident cattery cat: Ginger tom Orlando was a stray cat who wandered into Battersea's London home during the early 2000s and just moved himself in. He spent his days happily swanning around the Home and was never fazed by anything, not even the dogs.

Hadrian, the FIV+ Bengal: Hadrian ended up at Battersea Old Windsor after terrorising the neighbourhood's dogs and cats and breaking into people's houses through cat flaps. He was microchipped, but his owners didn't want him back for fear of legal action. It turned out that Hadrian was also FIV+ and so needed to be an indoor cat. After several foster homes, Hadrian finally found his forever home in Southampton.

Smokey, Battersea's pin-up boy: Smokey had spent most of his life fending for himself on the streets of Windsor before coming to Battersea Old Windsor. He soon settled in and became a soppy, lazy part of the family. He passed the time relaxing with staff in the cattery, greeting visitors and catching the odd mouse. He also appeared frequently in Battersea photos.

CATS
REMEMBERED

Cats lost, mourned and celebrated

Sharing your life with cats means paws, claws, head butts and the absolute
joy of a lap full of purrs. It also involves coming to terms with clothes that
are forever covered in hair, as well as, sadly, the inevitable loss. When people
die, there are time-honoured traditions and formalised rituals which guide
us through grief, but we're often at a bit of a loss to know how to mark
the passing of a much-loved pet. We may feel embarrassed at the depth of
our sadness and taken aback by just how difficult it can be to say goodbye.
Some people find the death of a cat so upsetting that they can't face having
another one. But grief is the price we pay for companionship and we can
honour and celebrate our pets in our own way, with poems or gravestones or
cherished memories or whatever it takes to get us through.

Do cats really choose to die alone?

It's often said that ailing cats go off somewhere so they can die alone. It's certainly not uncommon for elderly or frail cats to disappear and the assumption is that they have chosen to die somewhere quiet. But, as animals don't really have a concept of death in the same way that humans do, they are probably not consciously trying to find a place for a peaceful death. A cat's response to threat or danger is to hide, so when they feel ill they may seek out a safe space. It can be very distressing not to know what happened to your cat in their final hours or not even to find their body, but when we invite animals into our lives, we sometimes have to accept behaviour that is natural to them – however heartbreaking it can be for us.

A decent burial

The pet cemetery which claims to be the oldest in the world still to be operating is the Hartsdale Pet Cemetery in New York State. Originally called the Hartsdale Canine Cemetery, it opened in 1896, when a veterinarian allowed a friend to bury a much-loved dog in his apple orchard. The cemetery is the resting place of some 80,000 pets, including birds and reptiles, as well as the more usual cats and dogs.

There are also numerous pet cemeteries in Japan, where cherished companions can be cremated and their ashes placed in a small shrine, where photos, mementos, incense and even pet food are often placed. The Jindaiji Pet Cemetery in Tokyo is one of the city's oldest and largest. Around 20,000 pets, mainly cats and dogs, have been interred there in its fifty-year history.

Older, but on a much smaller scale, is the pet cemetery in Hyde Park, London, which began more by accident than design. When the dog belonging to a family who regularly visited the park died in 1881, the gatekeeper agreed to bury the dog in his garden. Before long, an unofficial pet cemetery began expanding in the small garden and by the time the cemetery was closed in 1903, around 300 little headstones had been squeezed in, including one for 'Peter, the faithful cat' and 'Ginger Blythe, a king of pussies'.

Paris has a much grander pet cemetery than London, complete with fine art deco entrance gates, and elaborate headstones and monuments to deceased companions. Le Cimetière des Chiens et Autres Animaux Domestiques (the Cemetery of Dogs and Other Domestic Animals) opened in 1899 in the north-east of Paris and is divided into four sections: one for cats, one for dogs, one for birds and another for other animals (where a lion, a racehorse, a monkey and some fish rest in peace). Among the cats buried at the cemetery is Kroumir, a beloved Persian who reportedly died of grief four days after the death of its owner, the author and politician Henri de Rochefort. Amid all this death, life goes on and the Paris cemetery is home to a population of feral cats who have their own 'maison des chats' for shelter and are looked after by a local cat welfare association.

Poetic goodbyes

'Who shall tell the lady's grief, when her cat was past relief?' Sounds like a job for a poet – and Christina Rossetti's poem 'On the Death of a Cat' certainly waxes lyrical about the passing of much-loved Grimalkin, who died giving birth to her kittens. It's not just a lady's grief that has been expressed poetically. Thomas Hardy wrote 'Last Words to a Dumb Friend', which eloquently expresses the great loss he felt when one of his cats was killed on a railway line. Less heartfelt is Thomas Gray's 'On the Death of a Favourite Cat, Drowned in a Tub of Gold Fishes', a parody of classical poetry which describes the unfortunate demise of a cat belonging to the poet's friend, Horace Walpole.

Can you leave all your money to your cat in your will?

Despite the occasional media stories about rich celebrities or wealthy animal lovers leaving huge sums of money to a favourite cat or dog, you can't actually leave anything to a pet in your will. As far as the law is concerned, pets can't own property because they are property. Leaving your fortune to a ginger tom is no more logical legally than leaving your pension fund to your garden or your collection of Siamese ornaments to your front room. What you can do, however, is set up a trust fund, which allows you to leave money or property to an individual or organisation on the condition that they look after your pet according to your wishes. Most pet owners worry about what might happen to their pets if they die and informal agreements between family and friends are common, but the only way to be absolutely sure that your pet will be legally protected after your death is to make your wishes clear in your will.

Gifts to Battersea

Around 35% of Battersea's donated income comes from gifts in wills. That's quite a sum, and the Home couldn't continue without it. In fact, without wills, Battersea would probably have never got off the ground in the first place – a legacy in 1863 allowed the Home for Lost & Starving Dogs to purchase the freehold of our first centre in north London.

Battersea also runs the Forever Loved card scheme, which gives peace of mind to members by taking care of cats and dogs should their owners die. Battersea can take in your pet and give them all the love and care they need while we find them a loving new home.

TEN CATS MEMORIALISED

Tom of St Mary Redcliffe:
Tom was the resident church cat
at St Mary Redcliffe in Bristol for
15 years. He was a respected ratter
and also accompanied the choir
into church on occasions. When he
died, he was given a funeral service
and his gravestone states simply
'The Church Cat 1912–1927'.

**Hodge, the lexicographer's
cat:** Samuel Johnson – poet,
critic, editor and biographer – is
best known for his work on *A
Dictionary of the English Language*.
His cat, Hodge, also has a place in
posterity and a statue of him can
be seen in London's Gough Square
bearing the inscription 'A very fine
cat indeed'.

Tiddles, the church cat:
Near the porch of St Mary the
Virgin in Fairford, Gloucestershire,
is a small headstone engraved with
the likeness of a cat called Tiddles,
who was resident there between

1963 and 1980. She regularly
attended services and sat on the
knees of willing congregants.

The cats of Thomas Hardy:
A little cemetery in the garden
of Max Gate, near Dorchester in
Dorset (where novelist Thomas
Hardy lived until his death in 1928)
is the resting place of a number
of pets, including numerous cats,
several of whom lost their lives on a
nearby railway line.

**Towser, the distillery
mouser:** The official mouser
at the Famous Grouse distillery
in Glenturret, Perthshire,
between 1963 and 1987, Towser's
extraordinary skill at vermin control
was verified by the Guinness Book
of Records and there is a statue
commemorating her achievements
in the visitor's centre.

Trim, the ship's cat: Born
aboard a ship in 1799, Trim went
on to become the first cat to
circumnavigate Australia (with a
little help from Captain Matthew

Flinders). Both captain and cat were imprisoned by the French in Mauritius on their return journey to England. Trim disappeared under mysterious circumstances during this captivity. There are several monuments to Trim in Australia, including a plaque in Sydney which features a memorial verse penned by Captain Flinders.

Mrs Chippy, the ship's cat:
Mrs Chippy (actually a male cat) was taken on board the Endurance during Ernest Shackleton's expedition to Antarctica by the ship's carpenter, Harry McNish. The cat was shot, along with a number of sled dogs, after the ship became trapped in ice. A life-size statue of Mrs Chippy was placed on McNish's grave in Wellington, New Zealand, in 2004.

Yelisei of Leningrad: During
the 872-day siege of Leningrad during the Second World War, many cats were eaten by the starving population. Consequently, the rat population exploded. Cats were brought in from outlying villages and the role played by these cats during this terrible time is commemorated with a statue to a cat called Yelisei in the city now called St Petersburg.

Wartime cats: The contribution
made by animals during the armed conflicts of the 20th century was recognised in 2004 when the Animals in War Memorial was unveiled in Park Lane, London. Alongside the horses, the mules and the carrier pigeons, the monument features a cat, in recognition of the work of feline rat catchers in the trenches and at sea.

Humphrey, the artist's
muse: A small statue of a cat called Humphrey sits on a plinth just in front of a children's playground in London's Old Gloucester Street. The statue was created by Marcia Solway, who studied sculpture at a nearby college where Humphrey used to hang out. The statue is actually a memorial to Marcia, who died tragically young at the age of 34 in 1992, the same year Humphrey the cat died.

THE TAIL END

Cats and humans have come a long way together since those days long ago
when cats first bravely but cautiously approached early settlements. Initially,
it was a relationship based on mutual self-interest. We'd inadvertently
made lovely homes for mice, which were much less appetising to us than to
cats. As rodents munched their way through our grain stores, cats saw an
opportunity too good to ignore and we were happy to have them around
so long as they made themselves useful. As they were perfectly suited to
their work, humans have done little to change cats. Even today, cats remain
remarkably similar to their wild cousins in both form and character.

It is this wild streak, coupled with an independent spirit and a natural
beauty, which makes cats so appealing to us today. Their affection can never
be taken for granted, which makes it seem all the more precious. These days,
we no longer depend on cats to keep our food stocks safe and we've largely
forgotten how important cats once were in their role as mousers. Now, of

course, cats are primarily companions, a position they have adapted to with astonishing success. Modern lifestyles can be something of a challenge for cats, which are naturally solitary and value their freedom very highly. Nevertheless, cats are now more popular as pets than dogs.

Despite our best intentions, however, humans don't always understand cats. Our feline friends, after all, experience the world from a totally different perspective and don't share our need for company. Fortunately, research into feline behaviour has come on in leaps and bounds in recent years and we're learning more and more about how we can help cats live happy, healthy lives alongside us. Just as importantly, cat owners increasingly see their cats as cherished members of the family and are prepared to go that extra mile to keep their cats content.

Legislation and changing attitudes have done much to alleviate the suffering of animals since the days when Mary Tealby first set up the Home, but, sadly, some cats are still mistreated or may find themselves without a home. Battersea Dogs & Cats Home has looked after over three million animals since it opened in 1860 and this vital work will continue as long as there are cats and dogs in need.

PICTURE CREDITS